THE FIFTH ACT

ALSO BY ELLIOT ACKERMAN

2034
(with Admiral James Stavridis)

Red Dress in Black and White

Places and Names

Waiting for Eden

Dark at the Crossing

Istanbul Letters

Green on Blue

THE
FIFTH
ACT

AMERICA'S END
IN AFGHANISTAN

Elliot Ackerman

PENGUIN PRESS   NEW YORK   2022

PENGUIN PRESS
An imprint of Penguin Random House LLC
penguinrandomhouse.com

Portions of this book originally appeared in a different form as "Winning
Ugly" in *Foreign Affairs* and as "The Botched Afghanistan Withdrawal Ex-
poses a Dangerous Fault Line in Our Democracy" on time.com.

MERCENARY SONG
Words and Music by STEVE EARLE
© 1994 WARNER/CHAPPELL MUSIC LTD.
All Rights in the U.S. and Canada Administered by WC MUSIC CORP.
All Rights Reserved
Used by Permission of ALFRED MUSIC
FOR OUR 100% CONTROL

Images pp. 6, 9, 12, 15, 18, 24, 33, 39, 56, 68, 74, 82, 96, 98, 114, 126, 134, 138,
149, 154, 162, 193, 254, 264, 266, 272: courtesy of the author; pp. 47, 49, 106:
courtesy of Matthieu Aikins; pp. 166, 167, 168, 171, 174, 224, 226, 227, 231:
courtesy of Chris Richardella; p. 185: from *The Washington Post.* © 2019 *The
Washington Post.* All rights reserved. Used under license; p. 196: photo by
WAKIL KOHSAR/AFP via Getty Images; p. 217: AF archive/Alamy Stock
Photo; p. 247: AP Photo/Malcolm Browne

LIBRARY OF CONGRESS CATALOGING-IN-PUBLICATION DATA
Names: Ackerman, Elliot, author.
Title: The fifth act: America's end in Afghanistan / Elliot Ackerman.
Other titles: America's end in Afghanistan
Description: New York: Penguin Press, 2022.
Identifiers: LCCN 2022007217 (print) | LCCN 2022007218 (ebook) |
    ISBN 9780593492048 (hardcover) | ISBN 9780593492055 (ebook)
Subjects: LCSH: Afghan War, 2001–2021—Evacuation of civilians. |
Paramilitary forces—Afghanistan. | United States.
    Central Intelligence Agency. | Afghan War, 2001–2021—
    Personal narratives, American. | Afghan
War, 2001–2021—Peace. | Disengagement (Military science) |
    United States. Marine Corps. Marine Regiment, 8th. Battalion, 1st. |
    Ackerman, Elliot.
Classification: LCC DS371.413 .A25 2022 (print) |
    LCC DS371.413 (ebook) |
DDC 958.104/745—dc23/eng/20220316
LC record available at https://lccn.loc.gov/2022007217
LC ebook record available at https://lccn.loc.gov/2022007218

ISBN 9780593653029 (international edition)

Printed in the United States of America
10 9 8 7 6 5 4 3 2 1

Book design by Daniel Lagin

For my friends,
alive and dead,
in these pages

Let a play which would be inquired after, and though seen, represented anew, be neither shorter nor longer than the fifth act.

—HORACE, *ARS POETICA*

CONTENTS

ACT I

THE
CONVOY
OF 109

Americans are asking: What is expected of us? I ask you to live your lives and hug your children. I know many citizens have fears tonight, and I ask you to be calm and resolute, even in the face of a continuing threat.

—PRESIDENT GEORGE W. BUSH
JOINT SESSION OF CONGRESS
SEPTEMBER 20, 2001

PROLOGUE

A hotel room, Rome, at night

The war has always been there, even though I don't go to it anymore. It is older than my children, who sleep in the room next door. I learned to love it before I learned to love my wife, who fits her body beside mine in the bed. The war is ending—has been ending for some time. And it is disastrous.

Kabul fell five days ago.

But even before that, my phone had begun ringing. The calls have built in urgency and followed me here, unexpectedly, on a long-planned summer holiday with my family. Today, I toured the sights with my children—the Colosseum, the Forum, the Baths of Caracalla. They complained about all the walking. They are too young to appreciate the ruins of an expired empire; still, I tell myself they'll remember walking these ruins.

5

All day, I lagged behind my wife and children, tapping out text messages, taking calls. I am working most closely with Nick, a friend and journalist who has organized a convoy of four minibuses for tonight. There are 109 people manifested on these buses. They are Afghan interpreters, activists, journalists. In the early morning hours, they will gather at the Serena Hotel in Kabul and board the buses for the airport. Another journalist has negotiated the convoy's safe passage through the Taliban's newly established checkpoints in Kabul. My job is to ensure the convoy's safe passage through the American checkpoints, specifically one gate at the airport. On the map, it is listed as the "Unnamed Gate."

Afghan paramilitaries are manning the Unnamed Gate. An old friend of mine, Jack, runs the CIA program that pays these paramilitaries. In our twenties, while in the Marines, Jack and I went through training together. He has made a career at the CIA and now oversees a vast network of paramilitary operations around the world. It takes me all morning to get through to him. Eventually, he returns my call. Hat in hand, I ask for his help. He deadpans, "I'm kinda busy right now." When I ask again, he says simply, "I'll see what I can do."

My wife's aunt, who has since passed away, was by all accounts a very glamorous woman and for many years was married to an equally glamourous Roman named Benito. That afternoon, once we'd finished touring the ruins, he came to our hotel with his daughter to meet us for a drink. Benito is in his nineties and was once ranked among the greatest professional bridge players in the world, winning tournaments from Monte Carlo to Las Vegas. We sit outside on the terrace overlooking the swimming pool. His memory is faded, but he wants to see the children, who play nearby chasing pigeons that peck the food from our table. Then Nick calls and I excuse myself. He explains that the US embassy has issued an advisory for an imminent terrorist attack at the airport. We debate whether we should postpone the convoy by a night. Nick isn't sure whether the Taliban will let us through tomorrow. All day long I've been trying to get some confirmation from Jack that our convoy will be allowed to enter the Unnamed Gate. Nick wants to know if I've heard anything else from him. How confident am I that Jack will come through for us? I tell him that I don't know. We decide to stick to the original plan and go tonight.

When I return to the table, my wife asks if everything is all right. I find myself apologizing to Benito and his daughter. I begin to explain what's going on, figuring there's no one they're going to tell. They listen attentively. Benito's eyes are upturned for a moment as if he is making calculations on my behalf. Then he says, "That is a difficult situation." His daughter frowns. A brief silence settles between us.

Now it's time to go. The buses are loading at the Serena Hotel. I'm monitoring their progress on my phone, in a chat room on Signal. I've gotten up from the bed where my wife sleeps, and I'm sitting at the hotel room desk. The lights of the city suggest themselves from behind the translucent curtain. Aside from that and the screen of my phone, the room is dark. Most of the passengers on the buses are strangers, but one family is not. My interpreter, Ali, and I fought alongside each other more than a decade ago in Shkin, a mud-walled firebase along the Pakistani border. Our Counter Terrorist Pursuit Team (CTPT) manned the southeasternmost outpost in the country. People called it "the end of the line." Our CTPT had T-shirts made up. Ali lives in Texas now. His mother and father in Kabul have received death threats from the Taliban, phone calls and a letter delivered to their house. They are on the bus, along with his two sisters, who, he reminds me, are "still young and very scared." Floating ellipses paired with the word *typing* often appear beneath his profile as he composes anxious messages that he never delivers; instead, he mostly responds to my updates with a simple *ok*.

The buses are leaving the Serena Hotel, 109 people in all.

Still no word from Jack. They are headed to the Unnamed Gate.

SCENE I

Fort Story, 2002

The sand hill was called Loch Ness. It rose out of the Virginia coastal flats like the hump on that mythical sea dragon. Every conditioning hike at the Marine Corps Amphibious Reconnaissance School—known as ARS—ended with a sprint up Loch Ness. The instructors watched us closely, and if you stumbled or your rifle touched the sand like a crutch, they would push you down the hill and tell you to start again. Temperatures hovered in the nineties that summer. More than once I vomited in the sand. Most of us did. Years later, a friend of mine who graduated the course kept a glass Coke bottle filled with Loch Ness sand on the mantel above his fireplace. He said he kept it there as a reminder for when things in his own life got difficult. Written in black Sharpie on the bottle was the word *Perspective*.

Jack and I met at ARS not even a year after 9/11. The war was new

then. No one understood how long it would last or where it would take us. We even worried we might miss it. I was a year from finishing college and had talked my way into attending the course, where we lived in a squat barracks atop the hill. Jack was about to take command of an elite force reconnaissance platoon. Every week or so, the instructors would give us a night or even a whole day off. We would drive into town in Jack's car, a beat-up, sand-brown Jeep Cherokee his parents had given him when he graduated college. Because I was only an ROTC midshipman and he was a commissioned officer—a first lieutenant—I called him *sir*. The Marine Corps is a funny place, the type of place where you call your friends *sir*.

Jack is a southerner, raised among the Blue Ridge Mountains. In college he minored in creative writing. He likes to talk about Faulkner and Walker Percy. He's a fan of the poet James L. Dickey. For years, Dickey worked in advertising. He wrote copy for Coca-Cola and Lay's potato chips while writing poetry after work. Later, Jack tells me something Dickey once said about writing poetry: "I was selling my soul to the devil all day and trying to buy it back at night." At ARS, Jack used to string a poncho around his bunk so he could read late into the night with a headlamp. He would keep his books stacked beneath his bed, alongside his combat boots. In Afghanistan, years later, guys would call him the American Pashtun. I think he liked this. He spent so much time in Afghanistan that the Musa Khel around Khost would eventually grant him tribal membership. Two decades ago, driving out the gate onto Route 60 toward Chili's or Applebee's, after days spent training in the Virginia woods, I remember the Steve Earle CD he would play. The album was 1995's *Train a Comin'* and the track was "Mercenary Song." It goes like this:

> *Me and old Bill there, we both come from Georgia*
> *Met Hank out in New Mexico*
> *We're bound for Durango to join Pancho Villa*
> *We hear that he's paying in gold*
> *I guess a man's got to do what he's best at*
> *Ain't found nothing better so far*
> *Been called mercenaries and men with no country*
> *Just soldiers in search of a war*
> *And we're bound for the border, we're soldiers of fortune*
> *Well, we'll fight for no country, but we'll die for good pay*
> *Under the flag of the greenback dollar*
> *Or the peso down Mexico way*

Neither one of us suspected our wars would go on for twenty years. That we would become like the professionals Steve Earle sang about. When the Taliban-led government refused to turn over Osama bin Laden after 9/11 and President Bush sent the first US combat troops into Afghanistan on October 7, 2001, it took only two months of fighting for the Taliban to collapse. The war—as we understood it then—had proven swift. The summer Jack and I met, the US-backed Islamic Republic of Afghanistan was formed, and even though bin Laden had escaped, the media was debating whether the time had come to declare victory in Afghanistan. This triumphal air soon vanished.

Of the many fatal mistakes made in our Afghan tragedy, the Bush administration would soon make the first: it would begin the war in Iraq. Within a year, Jack would be in Iraq leading a platoon during the invasion. Within two years, I would also be in Iraq, leading a platoon in Fallujah. Afghanistan is the older war, but for both of us Iraq was our first war; we deployed there first because Bush had made Afghanistan a second-tier priority. As the Iraq War raged, the lack of US focus in Afghanistan set conditions for the Taliban to reconstitute in neighboring Pakistan. By 2005, a Taliban-led insurgency reestablished itself in Afghanistan. President Bush's fixation on Iraq allowed this. What neither of us knew as we suffered through training in 2002 was that the Bush administration was laying an architecture that would sustain twenty years of war.

To wage war, America has always had to create a social construct to sustain it, from the colonial militias and French aid in the Revolution, to the introduction of the draft and the first-ever income tax to fund the Civil War, to the war bonds and industrial mobilization of the Second World War. In the past, a blend of taxation and conscription meant it was difficult for us to sustain war beyond several years. Neither citizens nor citizen soldiers had much patience for commanders, or commanders in chief, who muddled along. Take, for example, Washington reading Thomas Paine's *The American Crisis* as a plea to his disbanding army before they famously crossed the Delaware

("These are the times that try men's souls . . ."), or Lincoln, whose perceived mismanagement of the Civil War made his defeat in the 1864 presidential election a foregone conclusion to many, until Atlanta fell to the Union two months before the vote. The history of American warfare—even the "good" wars—is a history of our leaders desperately trying to preserve the requisite national will because Americans would not abide a costly, protracted war. This is no longer true.

After 9/11, in the opening act of the wars that followed, the Bush administration engineered a new type of war, one that is ahistorical—and seemingly without end. Never before had America engaged in a protracted conflict with an all-volunteer military that was funded through deficit spending. By the end of the Afghan War, our national debt hovered at around $28 trillion, with approximately $6 trillion being the bill for our post-9/11 wars, by far America's longest. In the aftermath of 9/11, there was no serious public debate about a war tax

or a draft. Our leaders responded to those attacks by mobilizing our government and military, but when it came to citizens, President Bush said, "I have urged our fellow Americans to go about their lives." And so, by the summer of 2002, as Jack and I were listening to "Mercenary Song," the war effort had already moved to the shopping mall.

For those who fight in a never-ending war, you must choose to leave it or to finish it. A decade in, when I made this choice, it nearly ended my friendship with Jack. And that night, in Rome, I wonder if he's forgiven me when I ask him for one last favor in Afghanistan.

SCENE II

Khost, 2011

The CIA base at Shkin is a satellite of Khost Base. The two are tucked into the high desert of the Hindu Kush. The CTPT that I advise in Shkin is several hundred troops strong. The CTPT at Khost is several thousand strong. For the past year, Jack has been riding a desk at Langley, having left the Marines for the CIA several years before. He oversees the schedule of who goes where in Afghanistan and when. He has taken good care of me and my career by placing me in Shkin. But his desk-riding is about to end. In a couple of months, he'll take over the mammoth task of overseeing what is—basically—a secret army at Khost Base. In preparation, he is flying in from the United States to get a measure of the place. When he takes over in a few weeks, I'm scheduled to be his deputy in Khost. I hop on a helicopter and fly an hour north from Shkin to meet him. The entire flight, I feel like I'm going to be sick, because I know that when I land, I am going to tell Jack that I'm not coming to Khost with him, that I'm leaving the war, that I'm done.

In the Marines, Jack was my big brother. Every place I served, he vouched for me. The summer after we'd met at ARS, I attended the Marine Corps Basic School in Quantico. When I arrived, Jack had already told his friends who were instructors that we'd gone to ARS together and that I would make a good infantry platoon commander. Later, at my first infantry battalion, he vouched for me with the staff noncommissioned officers, telling them that I was a solid, competent lieutenant. He did the same when I went to Marine special operations. When my formidable team sergeant, Gunnery Sergeant Willy "Bare Knuckles" Parent III from South Boston, called Jack to ask whether I was "a piece of shit or a good dude" (because you were either one or the other in that community and nothing in between), Jack again vouched for me, and shortly thereafter Willy and I got on famously. And, lastly, when it came time to leave the Marines, to head to the

CIA, he was already there, ready to place his reputation beside mine and vouch for me. He had hand-walked my application through Langley. Every time I thanked him, he would laugh it off, say it wasn't a big deal, that I was good at my job and so he wasn't doing me any favors. He would also say, "Someday we're gonna run this place."

And now we were about to run this place—or at least a corner of this place—by running Khost. But I was going to tell him that I wanted out, that I wanted a life outside these wars.

Again, I felt sick. Try as I might to rationalize it away, leaving the war meant betraying my best friend. It meant leaving him to fight on his own.

Every person who has fought in these wars and left them has had to declare the war over for themselves. Peace never arrived for us at a negotiating table or a surrender ceremony. There has been no single peace; rather, there have been tens of thousands of separate peace deals that each of us who walked away from the war had to negotiate with our own conscience. Like any peace deal, some have proven more lasting than others.

When I arrived in Khost that night, a raid was in progress outside the base. Because Jack would soon be taking over the unit, he'd tagged along as an observer. We kept odd hours back then. We'd wake up in the early afternoon. We'd go to sleep in the early morning. In the center of Khost Base was a little tiki bar, a Margaritaville transplant with a thatch roof and bamboo-legged stools. I perched on one of the stools and waited for the raid force to return. Not long after midnight, a convoy pulled into the motor pool. When the engines shut off, I could hear laughing and joking. Cleary, no one had gotten hurt. Maybe they'd even captured or killed their target. The Afghans left for their side of the base, and one by one the half dozen American advisers filtered past the bar, stripping off their body armor to reveal their sweat-stained uniforms.

I remained relatively new at the CIA. I'd met a couple of the other paramilitary officers at Khost before, but most I hadn't. Jack was quick to introduce me around. He was all jokes, recounting the particulars of the raid with the others—talking about who had jumped up on what roof, or had dipped around what corner, as they collectively chased their target down. Watching him, I could tell how much he'd missed this after his year at Langley. I could also tell how much he was looking forward to his time out here, running the vast CTPT in Khost, going out on raids like this almost every night. When he introduced me to the others, he said more than once, "Ack's gonna be deputy when I head out here."

Before too long, things at the bar wound down. One by one, everyone dispersed to their respective rooms for some sleep. That's when I asked Jack if he had a minute. There was something I needed to talk with him about.

"Can't it wait until morning, Ack? I'm beat."

I told him it couldn't.

SCENE III

The Colosseum, Rome, in the morning

I watch Kabul fall in my mother-in-law's kitchen, on a Sunday. I speak
to Nick shortly thereafter. He tells me he's raising money to charter
private flights out of Hamid Karzai International Airport, or HKIA.
Do you have any ideas on how to raise half a million dollars in a hurry? . . .
None come to mind. I ask how many flights he can get with all that
money. Just one, he explains, an Airbus A320. How many does that
carry? About 150, he says. I do the math, calculating dollars per seat—
trying not to remind myself that the real calculation being made is
dollars per life.

The calls keep coming in.

Another friend calls, a former Marine turned businessman. One
of his investors, a wildly successful tech entrepreneur, has a desperate
request. He's long sponsored the Afghan all-girls robotics team. He

needs to get them out, whatever the cost. I put him in touch with Nick. The entrepreneur commits to funding half a flight. Other commitments soon follow. Within hours, hundreds of thousands of dollars have gone to a first A320. The money seems to flow from everywhere—from Eric Schmidt, from the Rockefeller Foundation; people want to help.

That Thursday afternoon, I leave on vacation with my family.

When I land Friday morning, the problems have piled up. The issue now isn't flights but access to the airport itself. No one can get inside. The Biden administration has ordered the 24th Marine Expeditionary Unit to secure HKIA. Which they've done, to great effect. The North Gate, the West Gate, the Abbey Gate, they're all closed. When Jack returns my call about our buses going through the Unnamed Gate that night, I'm standing in the Colosseum gift shop with my two sons, who both want the same toy gladiator souvenir, and there's only one left. They're arguing as I answer the phone.

"Hey, man. What do you need?"

"Hey . . . hold on . . ." I run out of the shop. "Sorry, we've got these four buses and we need to get them to the airport tonight. I'm told your guys are holding security on the Unnamed Gate. We're planning to get there at 0330. Can you tell them to open the gate for us?"

"There's a lot going on right now," he says. "Do you even have a tail number for this flight?"

"Not yet." I had already talked to Nick about getting the tail number, and Nick had explained they wouldn't know that until the A320 was in the air. I tell this to Jack, assuring him that I can get the tail number soon. If he had that, would he be able to help us through the Unnamed Gate?

"Who's even on these buses?" he asks.

I mention Ali's family, the all-girls robotics team, journalists, activists.

"All right, but any Americans?"

I explain how a non-Afghan passport holder will be riding in each bus—we have four journalists: two Americans, a Canadian, and an Australian, who've volunteered to ride in the buses to help them through the Taliban checkpoints—but the four of them will be staying in Kabul. Only Afghans are flying out.

"And who are you working with on this?"

With each question, Jack's skepticism only grows thicker. I tell him about Nick, the Rockefeller Foundation, and our private donors. I promise I'll get him the tail number he wants. I'll send him the manifest of everyone on the flight. If he has all of that, will the guys at the Unnamed Gate let us through tonight? "I really need your help."

"That's not how it's working, Ack."

The line between us grows tense.

He answers, "I'll see what I can do," and hangs up.

My two sons come barreling out of the gift shop, each with a gladiator souvenir in their hand. My wife tells me the salesperson managed to come up with one extra.

SCENE IV

Washington, D.C., 2021

I was having lunch with Roya Rahmani, the Afghan ambassador, on the day President Biden announced the US withdrawal. She and I had become friends over the past couple of years and would periodically catch up over a meal. It was a simple coincidence we had lunch scheduled for that day. Her phone was ringing constantly as we stepped into the dining room of her residence. With a hospitality typical of Afghans, she sat us down at what turned out was a meal for one, as in observance of Ramadan she would not be eating. Then, as a steward brought my first course, her phone rang again. This call she had to take. It was the foreign minister. She excused herself as the two of them crafted a statement for her to deliver to the Biden administration. So I sat alone, picking at the vegetables on my plate, in what felt like a dream.

Two days later, I went for an early morning run with Jack. As we passed by the fenced-off Capitol and down along the National Mall, I recounted my lunch, how odd that moment had felt, and said, "I can't believe that's going to be my memory of how it all ended." Jack laughed, and with a doomy pragmatism predicted that the war wasn't going to end with a salad at the ambassador's residence and a news conference by the president; it would end as it began: in blood.

Jack reminded me that removing the 3,500 US troops from Afghanistan was, in military terms, what's called a "fighting withdrawal," in which an army leaves the field while still in contact with the enemy. Of all the maneuvers an army can perform (advance, flank, defend, etc.), it is widely accepted that a fighting withdrawal is the most complex and difficult because you are neither attacking nor defending, and so are exceedingly vulnerable. Unlike the withdrawal from Iraq, in which US troops could drive through the desert into Kuwait as they did in 2011, and unlike the Soviet withdrawal in 1989, in which they could drive across a then-shared border, US troops were marooned in Afghanistan, reliant on what were then three principal US-controlled airstrips (Bagram, Jalalabad, Kandahar), making their journey home all the more perilous.

Afghans have a long memory. During my service there, elders often pointed not just to where they'd fought the Soviets, or to where their great-great-grandfathers had fought the British, but even to the ruins of the fortresses where their ancestors had fought the armies of Alexander the Great. Perhaps the most famous fighting withdrawal in Afghan history came at the end of the First Anglo-Afghan War in 1842. That conflict began with a resounding British victory, in 1839, and the installation of a sympathetic government; but that government collapsed, leading to an uprising in Kabul. Like the United States and our allies, the British found themselves geographically marooned, and secured favorable terms for withdrawal from their adversaries, but when their column—around 16,500 soldiers and camp followers—left the gates of Kabul on their way to Jalalabad, the Afghans descended, slaughtering all except one: army surgeon William Brydon. When Brydon—the original Lone Survivor—arrived on horseback at the gates of Jalalabad, near death himself with part of his skull sheared off, a sentry asked where the army was, to which he responded, "I am the army."

Although the Soviet army avoided this fate a century later, the regime it left behind fared little better. Mohammad Najibullah, who the Soviets installed as president, was able to hold on to power for over two years after they left. As the Soviet Union collapsed, so too did their financial support of Najibullah's regime. He was soon deposed and eventually found himself at the end of a Taliban executioner's rope when they took control of Kabul. Which begged the question of how long the United States would support the government of then-president Ashraf Ghani. One year? Two? Three? What would be the "decent interval," to borrow Nixon's phrase from our calamitous withdrawal from Vietnam?

As Jack and I ran, we discussed this history and other complex aspects of America's withdrawal: how many senior members of the Afghan government possessed dual citizenship and would likely depart the country, leaving behind less capable subordinates to fill critical positions; the challenges of collapsing more remote outposts; and whether the State Department would expedite visas to those Afghans who'd thrown their lot in with their government and with us.

Jack concluded, "America might be done with Afghanistan, but Afghanistan isn't done with America." In his view, my lunch at the ambassador's residence wouldn't mark the end of the war at all. Not for me. Not for anyone.

That day at lunch, after finishing her call, the ambassador had apologized for being so inattentive. She confessed that she'd had an agenda item we hadn't gotten to discuss. She wanted some advice, as she was considering writing a book. Like the millions of Afghan girls the United States was now in the process of abandoning, her story was marked by war and overcoming an oppressive version of Islam championed by the Taliban, a personal journey that led to a final chapter in which she was appointed as the first female Afghan ambassador to the United States. My advice to her was to keep notes, and that she might not be ready to write the final chapter yet. Because she may not be remembered most for having been her government's first female ambassador, but rather for having been, as it relates to America, its last.

SCENE V

Gladiator school, Rome, in the afternoon

⸻

Nick has questions and Jack isn't answering his phone. Nick wants to know if our convoy has been cleared to enter the Unnamed Gate; if so, he wants to know what time we should arrive; he also wants to know if the charter flight has been cleared to land. He's asking questions that I don't have the answers to.

So I call Yeti.

Jack and Yeti work together. Yeti—as his name infers—is a bit of a giant. Before he played spook for the CIA, he played offensive tackle for a nationally ranked college football team. From his alma mater to the agency, he has many game-day stories he could regale you with, but he never would; he is modest to a fault, self-deprecating, and one of my favorite people. Like Jack, Yeti and I met in a training course years ago.

I explain the situation to Yeti and that Jack isn't answering his phone. Yeti offers to drive into the office to see if he can help. He also offers to send our manifest to the chief of Eagle Base, the main CTPT base in Kabul.

My family's tour that afternoon is finishing as I get off the call with Yeti. My wife and daughter have planned an excursion, and I'm in charge of the little boys. We have an activity planned. My wife has signed them up for gladiator school.

A taxi drops me and the two nine-year-olds off in a dusty, suburban corner of Rome. The school is advertised as having two sessions a day, in which the children will learn about Roman weapons and armor and then play gladiator with other children in a historically accurate reproduction of a gladiator school, or the *ludus gladiatorius*. Their website shows a green lawn, smiling faces, and staff who are happy to instruct your child in the finer points of mortal combat. When I push open the front gate, the reality is a cluster of one-story cinder-block buildings tousled with faux-thatch roofs built around an abandoned dirt courtyard. This is the *ludus*, and it appears deserted.

Our taxi has sped away; otherwise, I might've doubled back for it. I'm left to poke around inside. Then, out from one of the block houses, Claudio, the lead (and only) instructor, crosses into the center of the dirt courtyard. "Where are my gladiators?" he says with a ring announcer's panache. In each hand he carries a Roman short sword, the gladius. He clangs the two unsharpened blades together as if trying to detonate sparks. Both boys reach eagerly for the swords. "Ah, not yet," says Claudio. He thrusts both blades into the dirt so their upturned handles seduce the boys like an Arthurian legend—now he's really laying on the showmanship—and holds up his index finger. "First, you must learn."

Claudio's jogging shorts and tank top reveal his muscled legs and arms. Like a man in a bar before a fight, he sizes up me and then the boys from head to toe. He ducks into one of the block houses. He doesn't rummage around for long. When he reappears, he is dressed in leather calf-high sandals and an above-the-knee tunic belted at the waist. He hands each of the boys an identical crimson sackcloth tunic in their size and then offers me one in mine.

I explain that I'm not fighting today, only watching.

Claudio looks at the boys, who look at me. All three of them are disappointed. I hold up my phone. I'm expecting a call back from Yeti, and I explain how after that maybe I'll get in the ring for a bit. Then Claudio helps me out: "Come on, boys, leave your papa to his calls. Around the *ludus*! Warm up! Five laps!" Off they go running.

As I sit on the bench watching the boys do their laps in the dust, I'm taken back to when I'd told Jack I was done with the wars. That next morning, we had gone on a run. The night before, Jack had asked that I at least consider making one final trip with him to Khost. He asked that I sleep on my decision. So I agreed. When we met on the airfield for our run, it wasn't long after dawn. He confessed that he hadn't slept much. I confessed the same. We started out at a slow, silent jog.

"What would you even do?" he asked after a while.

I described to him a year-long job in politics that I'd been offered. After that, I wasn't entirely sure.

Cargo planes roared into the airstrip. A helicopter heaved up a dust cloud in the pastel distance. Static electricity crackled from its blades. We used this noise as a cover for our silences. Eventually, I told him that I hadn't changed my mind, that I wasn't coming with him to Khost. The silences became longer the farther we ran.

Eventually, he said, "I vouched for you."

"I know."

"You leaving so soon calls my judgment into question."

"I'm sorry."

"I'm not going to defend you."

I didn't have to ask, *Defend me against what?* I knew exactly what he was talking about. Our culture—the special operations culture I had aspired to be part of for so long and within which, up to this point, I had thrived—placed a heavy emphasis on personal reputation. This goes back to Willy asking Jack whether I was "a piece of shit or a good dude." There was and never would be any in between, not for me or anyone else. What Jack was telling me was that my decision to leave so precipitously—and particularly to leave him in the lurch in Khost— would probably cast me out of the "good dude" category, at least in the eyes of many. And he wasn't wrong. I knew some would view it that way. Most painfully of all, him.

We made a single lap around the airfield before quitting; it's the only run we never finished.

A year passed before we spoke again. Jack deployed to Khost without me, and it was only when he returned after a successful tour there that we gradually began to pick up our old habit of running together. We never spoke of my decision to leave. It remained buried between us: the right or wrong of it, the *how* and the *why*. We simply decided to let it go.

The boys have finished their laps around the *ludus*. Claudio passes each of them a juice box to cool off before he places a wooden sword in each of their hands. They begin a series of drills. Claudio chants, "Strike! Block! Recover!" as the two of them thrust clumsily at each other. When their energy lags, Claudio encourages them more earnestly. When this no longer works, he steps into one of the cinder-block huts with its shabby thatch roof. Then, from a constellation of concealed speakers around the arena, the theme from *Gladiator* begins to play. The strident melody. The epic drums. "Come boys!" he shouts. "Again!" And so they go on: *strike . . . block . . . recover.*

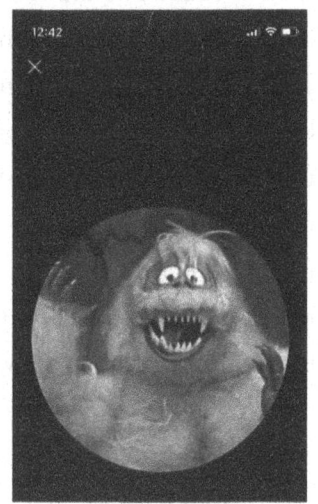

My phone rings; it's Yeti.

"What's that noise?" he asks.

Claudio's music is loud and so are the boys, whom he's now worked into a frenzy. I stopper my free ear with my finger and walk toward the gate of the gladiator school, apologizing to Yeti. "It's my kids. Can you hear me better now?"

He can and so begins, "I talked to Jack about your situation. Listen, man, I'm really sorry, but he asked me to step away. He said that he'd handle it."

"What does that mean?"

"I don't know. He just said he'd handle it and told me to step away." Yeti apologizes again. He confirms that he passed our manifest on to the chief of Eagle Base and that he wishes he could help more or get me a better answer as to whether our convoy is cleared for the gate.

He offers to let me know if he hears anything else, but aside from that there's little he can do.

Claudio is satisfied with the boys' progress. "Take a break from your phone," he tells me. "You will want to watch what comes next." Then he calls out to the boys, gesturing to the two swords he'd thrust into the earth at the beginning of the lesson. "Come, gladiators. Take your weapons." They run to the twin swords, their eyes widening when they feel the weight in their arms. "Face your father, our emperor. Hold your sword high and repeat after me: *Avē . . . Imperātor . . . moritūrī . . . tē . . . salūtant!*" When he asks the little boys if they know what this means, he's pleased that they both do. (They had, after all, spent the morning at the Colosseum.) Claudio doesn't waste any time as he continues his instruction. "Now, slowly, do as I taught you." He picks up his refrain of *strike, block, recover,* in a more restrained cadence. The boys swing the dull steel blades at each other, occasionally clanging their swords together.

I try Jack at his desk. His personal assistant answers. "He's in a meeting," she says. "If it's an emergency I can get him." I'm not quite sure how to answer. The hierarchy of emergencies in recent days has collapsed. Tonight, 109 people are going to load buses headed to HKIA. This bid for the airport is their last, best hope to escape a country that is about to descend into a political black hole. *So is it an emergency?* Yes, of course it is. But no more of an emergency than the myriad other issues Jack is contending with as Afghanistan falls, to include the evacuation of the many thousands of Afghan paramilitaries he's worked with during nearly two decades of war. What it really is isn't an *emergency* but rather a *favor*—yet another favor—from someone who has done me so many.

"If he could call me back, it'd be appreciated."

"Sure," she says. "I'll let him know."

The boys are really going at it now, flowing with their newly learned gladiator moves. Claudio, who is watching them closely to ensure no one gets hurt, flashes me a disapproving glance from over his shoulder. He raises his hands as though taking a picture with an invisible camera, as if to say, *Is your business call so important that you would miss this?*

To Claudio's delight—and my own—I focus on the boys, photographing them from every angle until they take a break. They sip water on the bench beside me and catch their breath. They're flipping through the photos I've taken when Claudio announces that time remains for one more battle. He tosses me the balled-up tunic I'd declined before. Evidently, this isn't up for discussion. Soon I'm dressed. When the boys reach for their steel swords, Claudio says that for this battle we will use the wood, practice swords. "Your father," he patronizingly explains, "doesn't have your training. He isn't ready to fight with the gladius."

The three of us face Claudio. He has us repeat, *"Avē Imperātor, moritūrī tē salūtant!"* And our combat begins. The boys, at nine years old, are on the cusp of having real strength, though they are not yet aware of it. When they hit me it hurts. More than once I have to tell them to take it easy. My half strength is no match for their full strength—and what type of father would fight his son at anything more than half strength? Claudio watches from the bench, shouting instructions to the boys and laughing mightily at me. In no time at all, I'm down on my knees. The boys have bested me. Their wood swords are at my throat. They look to Claudio, their emperor, for judgment.

His hand, thumb extended, hovers parallel to the ground. When he turns it up the boys groan.

"Come now," says Claudio. "Be fair. When a gladiator like your father fights well he should be rewarded. Do you know how the empire used to reward the best gladiators?"

One of the boys guesses gold. The other guesses a big house.

"No," says Claudio. "Nothing like that. They would reward him with something far greater: his freedom. So that he wouldn't have to fight anymore." Claudio steps into the arena. He offers his hand and pulls me up from my knees.

SCENE VI

Paktika Province, 2010

One of the last times I saw my interpreter Ali, we were driving through a valley in southeastern Afghanistan when a vehicle in our convoy struck an IED. An ambush followed. Muzzle flashes lit up the rocky hillside as we pried the bodies of four Afghan soldiers out of their mangled vehicle, including Mortaza, a friend of Ali's. I remember the two of us putting pieces of him in a black vinyl body bag.

Ali isn't his real name, but it's what everyone called him. To protect his family, he hid his identity. After I returned to the United States, Ali and I lost touch. But eighteen months before Kabul fell, I received an email from an unfamiliar account with the subject "This is Ali!" He told me that after several years of navigating the exhausting Special Immigrant Visa (SIV) program, he'd settled with his wife and children in Texas, where he was happy. He was worried, however, about his siblings and parents still in Afghanistan. They had received death threats from the Taliban because of Ali's work and that of his younger brother, also an interpreter who had been trying for years to get his own visa. We kept in touch after that. When the Biden administration announced its withdrawal, Ali wrote to plead for help in getting his family to safety. Tonight, they are on the flight manifest of 109 people.

My parent command when I first served alongside Afghan security forces was the Combined Joint Special Operations Task Force. Nearly a decade after US forces arrived in Afghanistan, its headquarters was still made of plywood, as were most of the other buildings that housed American troops. Resources existed to build out of concrete, but why would we do that? At any given point in our twenty-year Afghan odyssey, we were always—in our minds, at least—only a year or two out from a drawdown followed by an eventual withdrawal. Of course, the Afghans noticed this. At a remote outpost near the Iranian border where I was then deployed, the lead Afghan contractor who worked alongside my special operations team would always scoff whenever an aircraft brought in pallets of plywood for our construction projects. "Wars," he would say, "are not won with plywood."

On July 8, 2012, at a White House press conference, when Joe Biden was asked whether a Taliban takeover of Afghanistan was inevitable, he responded, "No, it is not. . . . Because . . . the Afghan troops have 300,000 well-equipped [soldiers]—as well equipped as any army in the world—and an air force against something like 75,000 Taliban. It is not inevitable." For years, Afghans like Ali and others in their country's security forces had been fighting their own civil war against the Taliban, sustaining casualties and holding ground. Their performance allowed US and international troop numbers to dwindle from nearly

150,000 at the height of President Obama's surge to 2,500 before the withdrawal without the total implosion of the country.

And yet these forces were shown to be a plywood army, one with the capability to accomplish the mission, but with foundational problems in recruitment, administration, and leadership. The Afghan military was, by design, a nationally recruited force, meaning that, typically, Afghan soldiers did not fight in their native provinces. Because of Afghanistan's history of warlordism, the decision to rely on a nationally recruited army (as opposed to a regionally recruited one) was made early on, in the Bush years; the idea was that an Afghan military without strong regional and tribal affiliations wouldn't threaten the authority of a central government.

This decision also had downsides. The tribal, familial structures that form the backbone of accountability in Afghan society did not transfer to its military. This created consistent disciplinary challenges within the ranks. It also proved a problem when waging a counter-insurgency. An ethnically Tajik Afghan soldier from Mazar-i-Sharif tasked to fight in heavily Pashtun Helmand Province would find himself as foreign there as any American. Once, when on patrol with Ali in a particularly remote corner of western Paktika Province—that, according to our records, no one from our firebase had ever visited—I recall the two of us lingering by our gun truck as the commander of our CTPT met with a cluster of village elders. Typically, on civically minded missions, we advisers would hang far back, doing our best to present an Afghan, as opposed to an American, face to our efforts. Noting how the villagers kept stealing wary glances at Ali and his Afghan counterparts—kitted out in their Merrell hiking boots and aerodynamic sunglasses—I wondered aloud if the villagers thought that *they* were Americans. "No," Ali said, laughing at my naivete. "They don't think that we are Americans." Then he cast his gaze out at the mud-walled compounds, some as tall as two or even three stories and layered like clumsily baked cakes. He surveyed the town a moment longer before adding, "They think that we are Russians." Had we managed to integrate tribal and regional loyalties into a national army, the Afghan security forces would have been built on a far stronger foundation, one in which Afghan citizens wouldn't have confused Afghan soldiers for Americans—or even Russians.

Aside from recruitment, the other areas where Afghan security forces proved endemically weak—administration and leadership—are closely linked. Slack in their administration—inaccurate troop rosters and incomplete equipment inventories, for example—has fed persistent corruption. Too often, as Americans, we equated corruption in Afghanistan with moral failure on the part of the Afghans, while rarely questioning our own complicity in setting conditions that fostered corruption. Most tragically, our consistent messaging that we were on our way out of Afghanistan encouraged Afghans in positions of power to embrace corruption—specifically, the siphoning of resources for personal gain—as the one clear and sure means of survival. Corruption became a financial contingency plan, the choice any reasonable Afghan would make to secure a safe future for their children. When every year the Americans promised that the next year would bring an American drawdown and eventual abandonment to the Taliban, ask yourself what choice you might make for your family.

Ultimately, the deterioration of the Afghan security forces doesn't occur on the battlefield as much as it occurs in the negotiating room, in which key tribal leaders (for example, Ismail Khan, whose switched allegiance delivered the entire city of Herat in the summer of 2021) either surrendered without a fight or cut deals with the advancing Taliban before any substantial battle for their cities might occur. The Afghan army is there, well-trained, well-equipped, and standing in the way of a Taliban advance, but in the end, it has no political leadership.

In Afghanistan, there is a saying: "The Americans have the watches, but the Taliban have the time." As far back as President Bush's decision to divert troops from Afghanistan to Iraq as part of the 2003 invasion, America has always had one foot out the door. Never once did we convince our allies—or our adversaries—that we possessed both the watches and the time. Ironically, this led to us spending more time in Afghanistan than we might otherwise have if we'd postured ourselves differently. Carl von Clausewitz, the great nineteenth-century military theorist, famously said, "War is the continuation of politics by other means." President Biden's announcement of a complete US withdrawal from Afghanistan set off a crisis of confidence among Afghans, one that precipitated a political collapse and, subsequently, a military collapse. The Afghan security forces might have possessed numerical and material superiority, but their belief in themselves evaporated when the United States and NATO withdrew the political and material support their government and military relied on. Does this result mean the Afghan government and military were irredeemable institutions, foreordained to collapse? To answer this, one might ask how the Taliban would have fared if, for instance, the Pakistanis had similarly withdrawn support. And if one believes the Taliban might have also collapsed, does this mean that their reliance on Pakistan similarly indicts them?

The ultimate disaster that unfolds in Afghanistan is the accumulation of hundreds of bad decisions over two decades. However, the one I can't seem to get out of my head is that we chose to build in plywood.

In the weeks before the fall of Kabul, Ali's requests for help had become more strident. He knew what was coming. What chance did his mother, father, and two sisters have when it had taken him three years to get his US visa? He'd had to gather letters of recommendation from past supervisors, submit to interviews, and undergo a medical evaluation. As the Taliban advance, the State Department is sitting on more than eighteen thousand unprocessed applications for visas. That June, the US embassy in Kabul locks down, not because of the Taliban but because of a COVID-19 outbreak. This halts all visa processing.

On June 4, a bipartisan group of twenty-one members of Congress, many of whom are veterans, deliver a letter to the Biden administration asking for an evacuation plan.

One of them is Representative Seth Moulton, an old friend from the Marines. "There is clearly no way to do this under SIV," he warns two months before Kabul's fall. "The US," he reminds me, "has managed such evacuations before. As the Vietnam War was ending, the US evacuated 111,000 Vietnamese to Guam in Operation New Life. America also evacuated Iraqi Kurds to Guam in the 1990s after the Gulf War. In both cases, once the evacuees arrived, the State Department vetted their applications for asylum in the US." The signatories to the White House letter believe the Afghans deserve a similar process. They call for extensive airlifts out of Afghanistan as well as temporary housing on the military base at Guam. Michael San Nicolas, the congressional delegate from Guam, commits to such an effort, despite concerns among his constituents about an influx of refugees fueling the spread of COVID-19.

Yet in the months before Kabul's fall, while there's still an opportunity to significantly expedite the visa process, or even begin a wider evacuation, the Biden administration does neither, fearing that an evacuation will only precipitate the Afghan government's collapse. The June 4 letter is met with silence. Representative Jason Crow, a former US Army Ranger and the other chair of the group, grows frustrated, telling me, "Our interpreters lived with us, fought with us, and some died with us. Without them, many of us also would not have come home." It's a sentiment shared by many veterans. Leaving those who worked with us behind will not just be a moral catastrophe; it will undermine American credibility abroad, a point the signatories of the June 4 letter address explicitly, believing the collapse is inevitable. "If we fail to protect our allies in Afghanistan," they write, "it will have a lasting impact on our future partnerships and global reputation, which will then be a great detriment to our troops and the future of our national security."

But the timeline for withdrawal has been set. The September 11 deadline has, since its inception, been arbitrary, of arguably no military significance, a gimmicky way to add symmetry to an otherwise asymmetrical conflict. As the withdrawal begins and the situation in Afghanistan deteriorates, the date is moved up, to August 31. If our back is up against a wall, it is a wall that we have built.

When I learn about the June 4 letter and its demand for a well-planned evacuation, I mention it to Ali on the phone. He doesn't say much. For the past three years, his younger brother has been trying to secure a visa. His brother is in Kandahar facing the Taliban advance, American troops having pulled out of the city in mid-May, leaving him and other former partners of ours behind. Ali tells me that his brother had recently sent him a letter by the Taliban, in which the group announced its plan to offer clemency to interpreters and those who worked for the Americans. "Really?" I asked. "Yes," he said. "So long as the interpreters repent and admit that they betrayed the Afghan people." When I ask what he thinks of the Taliban offer, he laughs and says, "These days, I'd hesitate to take anyone at their word."

SCENE VII

A hotel room, Rome, at night

The children are asleep in the adjoining room. The news plays on mute. The images from Kabul flash and go dark, flash and go dark. My wife dozes beside me. On Signal, I'm in a group chat with half a dozen others titled "Situational Awareness." It's everyone involved with getting out the group of 109—from those riding the buses to those coordinating our clearance through the checkpoints. The first message is posted at 2105 Kabul time when Nick writes, *Hey guys. This will be the space for our latest on the move.*

Over the next couple of hours, families begin arriving at the Serena Hotel in Kabul. They've been told to bring a single suitcase, nothing more. Attendance is taken in the hotel ballroom. A couple more hours pass. The group chat remains mostly quiet. Then Matt, a journalist who's riding on one of the buses because his Western passport should help the convoy navigate Taliban checkpoints, sends the following:

Recon car departing Serena.

A single sedan leaves the hotel, navigating the route ahead of the four buses to ensure that it's clear. We wait while the 109 are loaded onto the convoy. On a separate chat, Ali confirms with me that his mother, father, and sisters are now on a bus. He sends some optimistic emojis: a thumbs-up, two hands placed together in prayer. He also passes along the name of the senior CTPT commander at the North Gate, who by coincidence I know; it's Commander W., who worked at a CTPT adjacent to our own. This is good news.

Except I still haven't heard from Jack.

A photograph of the lead bus is posted on the chat for everyone's reference. It looks like the VW minibus in *Back to the Future*, the one that Libyan terrorists used to chase Marty McFly and Doc Brown through a shopping mall parking lot in the film's opening action sequence. To identify our buses for the Taliban and the CTPT paramilitaries, large yellow squares of construction paper are taped to the top left corner of the windshield. Matt writes, *I will be in the lead bus. Currently waiting at Serena for an update from scout car.*

Ten minutes later, Nick responds: *Scout car report "road is open until Unnamed Gate." @Elliot see map in situation report from Yeti.*

I reply, *Wait one.*

For a final time, I call Jack.

No answer. We don't have any choice but to go. I write, *When you get to the gate with the CTPT soldiers, the Afghan CTPT head is "Commander W." Feel free to use his name. That should help. I also have confirmation that our manifest has been sent to the chief of Eagle Base,*

the main CTPT base in Kabul. If you have any problems, also remind them that "This manifest has been sent to the chief of Eagle Base." All of that should do the trick.

The member of our team handling the Taliban checkpoints chimes in: *Matt, so you have the name—the chief of police we are in contact with is Hajji B. He's aware of the trip.*

Nearly an hour passes. We wait for the last of our passengers to load. My wife rolls over, exhales once sleepily, and asks me if they've left yet.

"Not yet," I say.

"Have you heard from Jack?"

"No, I haven't." I stare up at the ceiling, and then in an even quieter voice add, "And I don't think I will."

"You'll hear from him."

"I'm not so sure."

"Why would you say that?" She is awake now, sitting up with her back to the headboard.

"It's a lot to ask," I say. "If he orders his guys to open that gate, he becomes liable for every person let inside. All 109 on the manifest. He doesn't know these people. What if something happens? What if the Taliban or Islamic State use this convoy to infiltrate someone into the airport? That would come down on him. I'm asking him to take a professional risk."

"He loves you," she says.

"I know." And what I don't say, or rather what I don't need to say, is that I let Jack down once before. My wife knows about Khost. She knows that Jack and I have never really talked about it, that the incident remains buried between us. And I think she understands my fear that his silence at this moment is his way of indicating that our trust has never been fully repaired.

Matt sends a text: *Departing Serena. ETA Unnamed Gate approx 0330 local.*

I tell my wife the convoy is leaving. We are sitting in the bed, the phone placed between us, watching the texts roll in.

Ten minutes pass. The convoy is through the Taliban checkpoints.

Turned on 40 Meter Road, is the next update.

Nick, who is monitoring another chat, tells them to look for the Panjsher Pump Station. Matt replies, *Good, that's what we're aiming for. Turning off airport road by Uranus Wedding Hall.*

Matt writes, *Okay arriving in 5 minutes.*

Nothing from Jack.

Ali texts me on a separate thread. His family is sending him updates from the convoy. He's the first to alert me that they're stalled

at the Unnamed Gate. The CTPT is asking everyone to get out of the buses. Do I know what's going on? Are they going to be let through? On the convoy text chain, they're now exchanging tense messages. *Asking for passports.* We know not everyone has passports. I reply, *Offer your passports and reference the manifest.* Matt writes, *There's an American here,* to which I respond, *Is he helping?* At the back of the convoy, they ask, *Is everyone getting out?*

My wife asks how it's going.

"They aren't cleared. They're asking everyone to get out."

My phone pings with another text message: *Your buses just get to the gate?*

It's Jack.

Yes, I reply, *they're at the gate now.*

Ok. Just making sure.

"You all right?" asks my wife.

I show her the message from Jack. A minute later, my phone pings with another text message. It's from Matt: *Inside.*

Nick writes, *Can you confirm all four buses inside?*

Yep. Followed by, *Moving to airport now.*

Nice work, I write.

Then I send Jack a separate message: *All passengers in the airport.*

To which he replies only, *Congrats.*

Another message comes in from Ali: *What you and your friends have done for me is unforgettable. For the rest of my life, I will be grateful.*

Ali would've done the same for my family, which is my response, and then I set down my phone. "What's wrong?" asks my wife.

"Nothing."

"See, I told you that Jack loves you."

"It's not that," I say. I'm sitting with my back to her on the edge of the bed, and she wraps her arms around me like a cape. "I never doubted that."

"Then what was your doubt?"

I struggle to put words to it, and so offer a feeble, "I don't know."

Jack hadn't known any of these people. The only person he'd known in this was me. But he'd let all these people in anyway. And I hadn't known if he would. I hadn't known, after Khost and everything that we'd been through and all the things I fucked up and everything that we never said, if he would trust me that way again. I hadn't known if one last time he'd vouch for me.

ACT II

THE SECOND CONVOY

And as commander in chief, I have determined that it is in our vital national interest to send an additional thirty thousand US troops to Afghanistan. After eighteen months, our troops will begin to come home. These are the resources that we need to seize the initiative, while building the Afghan capacity that can allow for a responsible transition of our forces out of Afghanistan.

—PRESIDENT BARACK OBAMA
US MILITARY ACADEMY WEST POINT
DECEMBER 1, 2009

SCENE I

Shewan, Farah Province, 2008

An east-west road ran through the town. That road was a spoke off the Ring Road, which circumnavigates all of Afghanistan. We had driven through the night, south on the Ring Road, to get to that spoke. Since the afternoon before, our sister team had been fighting the Taliban on the far side of the town. Our convoy consisted of my Marine special operations team (about a dozen of us), a detachment of US Army special forces (also a dozen), and a company of Afghan commandos (around 120) spread through eighteen vehicles. We arrived at the spoke at around three thirty a.m. I pulled our convoy off on the shoulder of the road. We could see the east side of Shewan in the distance, a dark smudge through the green haze of our night-vision goggles. On the drive in, flares had popped up from outlier dwellings along the roadside—Taliban spotters marking our progress.

The town appeared quiet. My team's vehicles were near the front of the convoy. I radioed to the back of the convoy, to the vehicles that carried the special forces detachment. Our two teams—the Marines and the special forces—worked in tandem advising a newly formed battalion of eight hundred Afghan commandos. I was a captain, and my counterpart who led the special forces detachment was also a captain. His name was Dave, and I radioed him to let him know that I thought we should take our chances and push directly through the town; otherwise, if we tried to go around, we'd likely still be driving cross-country by the time the sun came up. One person always had to be in charge, and so mission to mission Dave and I would switch off who was the overall mission commander. Tonight, it happened to be my turn. But as a courtesy to Dave, I ran my thinking by him as we rolled the dice on driving through Shewan.

"Roger, sounds good," he said over the radio.

I rode in the back right seat of an armored Humvee. We'd ripped out the seat in front of me and filled the space with a suite of computers and several radios that allowed me to communicate not only with our convoy, but with aircraft overhead and our multiple higher headquarters, to include a Marine task force in Herat commanded by a major and the overall special operations task force in Bagram commanded by a colonel. In the driver's seat was our team's communication sergeant, Redbone, a ginger-haired and bewhiskered Marine who in appearance and demeanor resembled Garfield the cat. "Redbone, we're pushing," I said, as I clipped the radio handset back onto the parachute cord strung above my head; it held four other handsets attached to four other radios tuned to four other frequencies. Redbone turned over his shoulder. He sighed and floored the accelerator. We began our cannonball run through Shewan.

The town came up at us now, building in size and menace. Driving through one of these towns, the walls trap you in. There's no turning around and there's only one way to go, which is to barrel through.

The radio murmured static as we drove. We watched out the windows. The deserted shop fronts and the silent, mud-walled compounds outside looked like a vacant movie lot. Up in the turret, Brandon Langill—whom everyone called "Lang"—manned our truck's automatic grenade launcher. He rotated in the turret and his legs—which were the only part of him I could see—shuffled past. Lang was one of the younger members of our team. Blond-haired, blue-eyed, with an all-American, gee-whiz, midcentury demeanor, Lang loved, in no particular order: his mom, his dog, his hometown of Erie, PA, his high school sweetheart who taught kindergarten, meatloaf night in our mess tent, the craftsmanship of a finely balanced Benelli shotgun, the recoil of a .50-cal sniper rifle, and death metal. Before missions, he would often be in his room prepping gear—re-taping spoons on grenades, jamming rounds into magazines, tucking explosive breaching charges into pouches—his head nodding along to Megadeth or Slayer or Judas Priest with a placid grin. When he would see me, he'd glance up, offering a "How ya doin', sir?" To which I'd say, "Fine," and maybe ask, "You okay, Lang?" And he'd give me one of his neato Patrick Bateman smiles and say, "Great!"

Buttoned up in the Humvee, it was hard to see. I shouted up to Lang in the turret, to ask him how it was looking. "Quiet," was his response. Our team sergeant, Willy—or "Bare Knuckles," as he was affectionately known—came up on the radio, confirming that from his vantage point it was the same: quiet. If Lang's warm, wholesome demeanor belied an inner killer instinct, the opposite was true of Willy. Externally, Bare Knuckles was all killer instinct. A fifteen-year veteran of Marine special operations with multiple combat deployments under his belt, he dispensed profanity as punctuation. *Fuck, shit, cocksucker* became proper nouns when spoken by Willy. In no particular order, he loved: Jack Daniels; Marlboro Reds; Redbone's stash of porn; his motorcycles; his wife, Yvonne; and his stepson, Chris, who he raised as his own and who a decade later would follow him into the military. He also loved me, and I knew this because he was fiercely loyal not only to me but to everyone on our team. As with Lang, I'd also swing by Willy's room before missions. While prepping his gear—jamming mags, rechecking the convoy route, tucking explosive charges into pouches—he'd typically have a winsome air about him. With a cigarette dangling from his lips, often shirtless and wearing a folded red bandanna as a headband, he'd loop a CD of Andrea Bocelli's "Con te partirò," which he'd sing along to. On seeing me, he'd glance up and typically offer a "You ready for this one, skipper?"

Tonight's mission had come unexpectedly. A six-hour drive south of us, our sister team had responded to an attack on an Afghan police checkpoint outside of Shewan only to find themselves in a running gunfight with the Taliban. It had gone on all yesterday before they eventually asked us to reinforce them. As our blacked-out convoy threaded through Shewan without incident, I switched over to our sister team's internal frequency. I tried to raise them on the radio but without luck. Redbone, seeing the difficultly I was having, leaned over. With one hand on the steering wheel and the other toggling radio switches, he managed to troubleshoot my problem. The other team came up on the net. They turned on an infrared strobe, and I was soon able to pick them out in the distance. A seam of light was forming the horizon as we arrived at their makeshift bivouac, which was little more than a circle of Humvees, with machine guns, grenade launchers, and sniper rifles swiveling their snouts around, sniffing for some hidden threat.

Little reunions commenced among the Marines as we piled out of our vehicles. Our special operations company was spread throughout western Afghanistan, and it was rare for Marines on different teams to see one another. In addition to our sister team, part of our company's Herat-based headquarters was there, to include our air officer, Captain Garrett "Tubes" Lawton. Indefatigably upbeat, Tubes found me in the now-fading darkness. He snuck up from behind and grabbed me in

a bear hug, lifting my boots off the dirt. "Leeeroy Jenkins!" he bellowed, referencing an obscure meme from the *World of Warcraft* video game, of which he was a fan. (If you want a laugh, google Leeroy Jenkins.) When I turned around, I pointed at him and asked, "What's that shit growing on your lip?"

Most of us had beards, but Tubes had decided to double down on a Fu Manchu–style mustache instead. He pinched one end villainously and said he was glad that I liked it. Tubes had come to us from Marine Fighter Attack Squadron 224, the Fighting Bengals. He'd earned his call sign, Tubes, after a night of raucous drinking that ended with him intubated in a Beaufort, South Carolina, emergency room. In his squadron, he'd flown in the back seat of an F/A-18D Hornet as a weapons systems officer. He was beloved. Our company had cliques and rivalries. Tubes floated above all of that.

He'd been with our sister team for some of yesterday's fighting. He pointed to a smattering of curry-colored dwellings in the middle distance. The Taliban had scooted into these interconnected compounds yesterday afternoon. Tubes had kept a surveillance drone hovering overhead most of the night. No one had left, he said. Dave joined us and we reviewed the plan for the coming day, which was breaking all around us only to reveal the compound walls pockmarked by bullet holes that attested to the ferocity of yesterday's fighting. The team we'd come to reinforce was exhausted. Our force of two teams plus commandos was fresh, even though we hadn't slept. We would go clear out the compounds. Each of our vehicles had crates of ammunition in the back, including grenades, rockets, and plastic explosives. To distribute the ammunition, Dave called up his team's weapons sergeant, who was also named Dave. Of the dozen members of Dave's team, three were named Dave. Dave, the team leader, was known as "Super Dave," while Dave the weapons sergeant (a notorious curmudgeon) was known as "Angry Dave," while the third Dave, Dave Nunez, wasn't known as Dave at all, but rather "Momez." The story went that after a night of drinking to celebrate the end of a training exercise, Dave Nunez had passed out on the group sergeant major's cot. When the sergeant major called Super Dave to say he had one of his soldiers, Dave Nunez slurred his own name so badly that the sergeant major heard it as "Momez," and so the sergeant major cussed Super Dave out, telling him to get his ass to headquarters and pick up Sergeant First Class Momez.

While Super Dave and I finalized a plan to clear out the compounds, everyone else in our two teams—including Willy, Lang, Angry Dave, Redbone, and Momez, to say nothing of the 120 Afghan commandos we advised—loaded up on the ammunition we'd need to clear out what we believed to be around two dozen Taliban fighters. On a tablet, Tubes continued to monitor a live feed from the aircraft hovering overhead. He confirmed that no one had left the compounds.

The Afghan commandos dispersed in a line of advance, their NCOs and officers haranguing them into position. It was late morning. The sun was a quarter of the way up in the sky and right in our faces, making it difficult to see the rooftops and windows to our front. The first shots would likely come from those hiding places. Weighed down with the grenades, rockets, and explosive charges that we would need to fight house-to-house, it made little sense to rush our approach. We'd only be exhausted once we got there. And so we came on steadily.

As we advanced over the uneven ground, Willy hustled up beside me. He placed his hand on my shoulder. "You ready for this one, skipper?"

SCENE II

A train from Rome to Venice

Tonight, we're going to try to do it again. Nick has already made a new chat on Signal: "145 out of Serena Hotel." The plan is the same as last night, with certain differences. First, it's more people. This shouldn't be a problem. Last night, the buses weren't entirely full, but tonight they will be. Again, we'll depart from the Serena Hotel. Another group, one sponsored by the Qatari government, is also going to be at the hotel. It was inevitable that others would use the hotel as a staging point, but this influx is something we'll need to keep an eye on, lest our two groups intermingle. The Taliban checkpoints shouldn't be a problem either, though you never know. With regard to the American checkpoints, I've exhausted my favors with Jack. We'll need to find someone else to open the gate at the airport.

I'm working over these particulars in the group chat when my eleven-year-old daughter, who is sitting next to me on the train and looking out the window, says dreamily, "It's hard to imagine."

"What's hard to imagine?" I ask.

"That the streets are going to be made out of water."

This isn't the first time we've had this conversation. At eleven, she's fascinated by Venice. "You're going to see it soon."

"Do you think people who have only ever lived in Venice find it hard to imagine normal cities, ones where the streets aren't made of water?"

"I don't know. What do you think?"

She stares out the window, so that when she answers she's not addressing me so much as the view outside. "Someone might have seen pictures or videos of regular streets, but I don't think that'd matter. It'd still be hard to imagine what to everyone else seems normal."

My daughter's gaze remains fixed out the window. A few more messages come into my phone; specifically, ones from Ian, an old friend of mine from the Marines and CIA who's now helping with the gates at HKIA. He has a contact in Senator Tom Cotton's office. Senator Cotton sits on the Senate Select Committee on Intelligence, and this contact of Ian's believes that the senator can get CIA to grant us the required clearances for our convoy to pass through the Unnamed Gate. While we're working out the details on the group chat—the information required in our manifest, the precise time the convoy needs to arrive at the gate, the tail number of the charter flight out of HKIA—my thoughts return to what my daughter said about the strangeness of trying to imagine a place where the streets are solid if you've only lived in a place where they're made of water.

People have, from time to time, asked me about the difference between serving in Afghanistan and Iraq. In Iraq, the war had only been going on for a few years. The conflict was a disruption to the status quo. Most Iraqi civilians desperately wondered when peace would return and they might resume their normal lives. This was not the case in Afghanistan. When I served there, the average life expectancy for an Afghan was around sixty years old. This meant the generation dying off were young adults when the Soviet Union invaded in 1979, while more than half of the population hadn't even been born. For Afghans who remembered peace, it was a dim memory, and for most Afghans there was no memory of peace at all. For most Afghans peace was not about returning to a condition that once was; for them peace was an act of imagination.

Lieutenant Colonel Jabbar, the commander of the Afghan commandos, never talked about peace, and I doubt he ever imagined it. Whenever I've since tried to imagine Afghanistan at peace, Jabbar has inconveniently come to mind. He never fit in the picture. A veteran Tajik commander, he'd spent twenty-five years at war against the Soviets and then the Taliban. What place could Jabbar hold in an Afghan society without war? This is what I struggled to imagine. When I first met Jabbar, the two of us had needed to travel across Afghanistan on US military aircraft. We were preparing to move his battalion from where they'd been training outside of Kabul to their new base in the west of the country. Like the legendary Kareem Abdul-Jabbar, he was exceedingly tall, well over six feet, and stood out in a crowd. Jabbar's English was spotty, and aside from a few phrases my Dari was nonexistent; the absence of an interpreter led to long, awkward silences on our layovers at many a small airstrip. Eventually, we needed a way to pass the time, so we took to playing chess. Because of his conspicuous height, Jabbar often drew curious onlookers who would linger over our games. When Jabbar won—as he inevitably did—my fellow service members, having underestimated his abilities, would stare dumbfounded as he slotted in his checkmate, knocked over my king, and chuckled while shaking his head: "Ha, ha, ha . . . *my* adviser."

I have, in recent days, been wondering what Jabbar would think about our harried withdrawal from Afghanistan. I have imagined him stealing away to the northeast, to the Panjshir Valley, to take up resistance along with other Tajiks in a reconstituted Northern Alliance under the leadership of Ahmad Massoud. Or perhaps Jabbar died alongside his commandos, in a desperate rearguard action, a last bid to stall the Taliban advance. I don't know. And I likely won't hear. Jabbar wasn't the type to keep in touch. Still, I wonder what he would think about the US presence in Afghanistan being reduced to a flimsy perimeter around Kabul's international airport. I wonder how he thinks the coming days will end.

Nick calls. He wants to know how confident I feel about Ian's contact in Senator Cotton's office. Do I think they'll be able to get the gate open for us? I joke that I feel about as confident as I did the night before. Which isn't very. I tell him, "I think a coin toss is the best we can hope for."

"I guess we'll keep using the Unnamed Gate until it stops working," he answers. I can hear the fatigue in his voice. Neither of us slept more than a couple of hours last night, and tonight promises more of the same.

"Then what'll we do?"

"I don't know," says Nick. "We'll have to figure out something else."

"You know this doesn't end well."

"What's that supposed to mean?"

Our efforts, along with those of others, are rooted in some broader ethos of leaving no one behind. Nick never served in the military, but if you've spent any time immersed in that culture—as Nick has—you quickly come to understand how deeply this ethos permeates it. But ultimately, this evacuation is going to end with us leaving allies behind. We know that, and so when I say, *This doesn't end well*, that's what I mean.

"Let's just get the gate open tonight," Nick says.

I continue to monitor the group chat. Before long, my thoughts have returned to Lieutenant Colonel Jabbar and one specific chess game of ours. It occurred toward the end of our time together, and it's when I finally beat him. It was just the two of us in his office one night playing, and he was completely taken off guard by my win. Having grown a little arrogant, he wasn't giving our game his full attention. When I knocked over his king, it surprised him, and I mimicked his chuckle, which so often I'd had to endure, saying, "Ha, ha, ha . . . *your* adviser." He was—as grizzled Afghan colonels go—a remarkably good sport about it. But the next day, after our morning staff meeting, when we had our interpreter with us, he pulled me aside to raise one objection. He conceded that he had lost the game the night before but took exception to the idea that I had, in fact, beaten him. "You must understand," he said. "What happened last night was that I beat myself."

Our train pulls across the lagoon, arriving at Santa Lucia station. I wake up my daughter, who's leaned her head against the window. She rubs her eyes with two fists and, blinking, sees Venice for the first time. Everything is luggage and crowds in the terminal. Eventually, we find a water taxi outside the station, on the canal. The taxi gently

pitches and sways in the wake of passing boats. After loading our bags, the pilot offers my daughter his hand. She climbs into the taxi and chooses to sit by herself in the stern. As we pull out onto the canal, I glance back at my daughter. When she thinks no one is looking, she dips her arm over the gunwale. She traces her fingers through the water.

SCENE III

Shewan, Farah Province, 2008

We cleared house-to-house and room-to-room. We didn't find anything. It seemed the Taliban must have vanished into the countryside
during the night. Tubes remained skeptical. For hours, he'd had aircraft stacked overhead watching this cluster of compounds. No one
could have escaped without us seeing them. Our sister team had
spent all of the prior day fighting the Taliban and so wanted us to
keep looking. The idea that the Taliban would simply vanish was a
bitter pill for them to swallow. So, to appease our comrades, we continued our search, though it had become obvious we weren't going to
find anything.

"How much longer are we supposed to keep this up?" asked Willy.
He was standing in the midday sun, leaning against an exterior mud

wall. He'd soaked his headband in bottled water and was putting his helmet back on. Next to him stood a turbaned man and his family who we'd turned out of their home. A half dozen commandos were searching it for a second time. Whenever a noise came from inside—the slam of a door, the sound of an item crashing to the floor—the man would shout at Willy, who only grew more irritated. I told Willy that we'd give it another twenty minutes. To get back to our firebase, we still had an eight-hour drive. No one had slept and I was keen to get our convoy home safely without anyone nodding off behind the wheel.

By the time we walked back to our vehicles, it was early afternoon. The sun was at its height and moods had turned short. We'd entered the town loaded for bear, with each of us carrying an extra fifty or sixty pounds of ammunition, none of which we'd used. Carrying it had worn us out. We now had to repack that ammunition. Redbone grumbled unintelligibly as he and Lang wedged extra rockets and plastic explosives into the back of our Humvee. As we worked on our truck, Tubes pulled up beside us in his. He was headed back up to Herat and wanted to convoy with us to our firebase, to spend the night, and then to make the rest of his journey the following morning. I told him to pull in behind Super Dave's last vehicle. "Which one's that?" he asked. I pointed to Momez, who was standing in the armored bed of the truck, stacking and restacking rockets, crates of grenades, and machine gun ammunition. He couldn't quite make it all fit.

As Tubes pulled in behind Momez's vehicle, Super Dave came over to mine. He stuck his head in my door, and we squinted at the mapping software on my laptop while we discussed the route home. Shewan stood between us and the Ring Road. If we went cross-country, around the town, it'd add another three or four hours to our drive. We wouldn't get back to our firebase until early the next morning. That would mean asking our drivers to go seventy-two hours with no sleep. "If we do that," said Dave, "someone's going to nod off and crash." I didn't disagree with him. Everyone was exhausted. If we went straight through Shewan, we'd save that time. The aircraft Tubes had orbiting overhead had been watching the town. It had reported no unusual activity. Going through Shewan seemed a safe enough bet.

We pulled onto the road, a single cracked ribbon of asphalt that would take us east to the more smoothly laid Ring Road, and then north to our firebase. It's a challenge to keep a large convoy together. The addition of Tubes's two Humvees, tucked behind Super Dave's in the back of the column, brought us to a total of twenty vehicles and right around 180 people, or *pax*, a count that Willy called over the radio as we departed. I kept the pace slow at first. Eventually, Super Dave called up from the back. All vehicles were on the road now. I sped us up to about thirty miles per hour. Any faster would've caused our convoy to accordion, placing gaps between the vehicles.

The heat. The whine of the engine. The lulling rhythm of the Humvee. I could feel myself nodding off as we approached Shewan. I reached into my cargo pocket and took out a piece of gum, hoping it might wake me up. A little under an hour later, when we got to the outskirts of Shewan, I was onto my third piece. The town, which sat low and indistinct on the horizon, quickly took shape as we drew closer. A market bracketed the main road. Brightly painted aluminum doors fronted the shuttered stalls. Hastily parked cars littered either side of the road. As it had when we'd passed through before, an atmosphere of abandonment lingered about the town; except now it wasn't the middle of the night but rather the middle of the day.

From inside the town, a tanker truck shot out onto the road. It hurtled toward us. Lang's steps orbited in my direction as up in the turret he trained the barrel of his automatic grenade launcher onto the tanker. Then the tanker stopped. Slowly, it began to make a three-point turn, blocking our way and causing our convoy to bunch together. Our lead vehicle, a Ford Ranger pickup driven by the Afghan commandos, pulled beside the tanker. The commandos yelled at the driver, gesticulating wildly, waving him off the road. They leveled their machine gun at the cab. The driver, however, remained indifferent. I could see him through his windshield, calmly working the gearshift. His gaze was cold, expressionless. He wouldn't be hurried. Something about him made me pick up the radio. "Everyone, keep your eyes open." A shudder went to the roots of my hair.

I thought to turn us around, but we were committed. Our first few vehicles—including mine—had already penetrated the outskirts of town. The idea of reversing the entire convoy seemed even riskier. We were already in range of whatever threat existed inside Shewan.

Another few seconds passed. The tanker finished its turn and sped into town, driving unreasonably fast, as if wanting to place as much distance as possible between itself and us. We got underway again, the front of the convoy starting out slowly, allowing the back to catch up. The commandos in front of us, who sat anywhere between four to six in the bed of their pickups, appeared especially vigilant. They kept their profiles low as we entered the town, crouching behind their rifles. Everyone could feel it. In those seconds we knew. The shuttered storefronts. The deserted streets. The glimpse of a woman grabbing a child off the street. It was so obvious as to be cliche, as foretold as any high-noon scene in a spaghetti western, as apparent in life as it would have been on the screen when, say, the tumbleweed blows through town, when the gunfighter cocks both his pistols and walks out in the street. You know that it's coming.

The first rocket-propelled grenade went wide. Fired from the north side of the street, it sailed overhead. I reached for the radio, and Lang swung left in the turret, stepping on my arm. "Contact left, RPG!" I shouted into the handset. Then, doing my best to sound calm and level, I added, "Near ambush, all vehicles push through the kill zone." Above my head, Lang had gotten to work, jackhammering out three- to five-round bursts from the automatic grenade launcher. Each 40 mm round is the size of an egg, and the recoil caused our Humvee to lurch to the right. Out of the corner of my eye, I could see Redbone tugging the steering wheel left while he floored the accelerator. Tactically speaking, there's only one rule when caught in an ambush: *Get out of the kill zone.* In Shewan, the Taliban had turned the length of this road into a kill zone.

Muzzle flashes winked from the windows. Light and medium machine guns knotted the air, swirling up whippets of dust with their recoil. An RPG slammed into the bed of the Ford Ranger in front of us. It failed to detonate but still tore off the tailgate and knocked one commando unconscious. The RPG gunner, a teenager with a wispy beard, clad in all black except for a dirty pair of white running shoes, vanished in a pink mist. I patted Lang encouragingly on the leg while he cursed and manhandled his turret to his next target, a building up ahead. He chomped a bite out of its side with another burst of grenades. Redbone, ever the multitasker, drove with his left hand while balancing the barrel of his shotgun on the ledge of his window and firing it with his right. Our Humvee began to swerve side to side after the Taliban shot out two of our tires.

Then everything quieted down.

The open desert presented itself to our front.

We pulled onto the shoulder of the road. Behind us, thick, acrid columns of black smoke towered upward like monuments. A first and then a second of the commando vehicles sped out of the kill zone. The Afghans perched in the beds of these trucks remained rigid and unmoving in their firing positions, all twitchy looks with eyes throttled wide-open. Next should have been a pair of vehicles, to include Willy's—but behind was only the vacant road.

Then, sputtering up through the hazy distance, came one Humvee

towing another. This was the last of our team, but not the last of the convoy. Remaining in Shewan were about half of the commandos, all of Super Dave's special forces detachment, as well as our headquarters. Willy pulled up beside us. He stepped stiffly out of his truck, which had eaten an RPG, while the Marines inside now dipped into their first aid kits to plug the little holes from which they bled. I stood outside my Humvee, holding a radio handset to my ear as I passed along a situation report to our higher headquarters at Bagram Air Base. Willy rinsed out his eyes and mouth with a bottle of water as he approached, still choking a bit on the smoke he'd inhaled in the ambush. I told him that I needed a head count.

"I'm working on it," he said, hacking between sips of water. He then pointed to the dashboard, where I'd left my pack of gum. "Can I have a piece?" I handed Willy the pack. I realized that I needed a piece too. In the ambush I had swallowed my gum.

From the outskirts of Shewan, the Taliban continued taking pot-shots at us. We worked with the urgency of a pit crew, changing shot-out tires on a vehicle while turret gunners like Lang returned fire into the town. In ones and twos, the remainder of our convoy passed through the kill zone, limping toward safety. Willy now had a head count. We had all but two vehicles. That's when we spotted a last Humvee staggering up the road. Piled on its roof and hood—and clinging to it like a life raft—were the remaining members of our convoy.

Super Dave had already arrived when this last Humvee rolled in. He had been helping Willy with the head count. This was the nineteenth vehicle out of twenty. There was some confusion as to what had happened to the twentieth. While Dave and Willy tried to figure out if this was everyone, Tubes hopped off the hood. Flames had singed the corners of his mustache and his eyebrows and had charred his sleeves up to the elbows. The skin beneath was dazzled with burns and hairless. It shined like polished stone. He interrupted everyone's counting: "We're missing one," he said. "Momez is still back there. He's dead."

SCENE IV

A hotel room, Venice, at night

I am lying in bed. My phone is balanced on my chest when the message *Buses rolling* comes across the group chat. Earlier in the evening, a flight's worth of evacuees organized by the Qataris had delayed us by more than an hour, causing confusion at the Serena Hotel. We'd almost called off this night's evacuation because of it. But at the last minute the Qatari group had gotten on the road to the airport. This had given us enough time to load onto our own buses. Matt, who is riding on the buses again, posts *ETA 0430* in the group chat as our convoy gets underway. Like last night, we don't yet have confirmation that the CTPTs at the Unnamed Gate will allow us to enter. Still, we roll the dice that Ian's contact in Senator Cotton's office will come through.

Communications in the Signal group are crisp, professional. Matt: *Turning on 40m rd.* Nick: *copy.* Matt: *Airport rd.* Nick: *copy.* There's a confidence tonight that wasn't there the night before, even though most of us in this group have never met one another, or the Afghans we're trying to help.

Before dinner, my wife had encouraged me to explain to the children what was happening. They could tell I was distracted and increasingly tired. She knew these evacuations would continue and thought it better to explain the situation to them, lest they wonder what was going on with me and worry. "They're old enough to understand," she'd said as we unpacked in our room. We ate in the hotel restaurant, which was in a garden. My daughter wore a dress. The boys wore collared shirts. There was the water of the lagoon in the distance, a breeze, and the light of the city reflecting off that water.

"We know," said my daughter. "It's Afghanistan." When I asked her *what* she knew, she said, "You're trying to help people leave because we lost the war."

My son interjected, "When Dad left, we were winning the war."

"Not really," I said.

"Then we were losing when you left?" my son asked.

Again, I answered, "Not really." I'm not sure whether we were winning or losing when I left. This was in 2011. It was at the height of Obama's surge, an effort that was doomed from its inception two years before, when the president announced both the increased troop levels and the date for our drawdown in the same speech. Doing this was a hedge on Obama's part, a way to appease the hawks with a surge and the doves with a withdrawal. But it proved a hedge that caused the Afghans to hedge in turn. In countless meetings with tribal leaders, district mayors, and provincial officials, the content of Obama's speech would come up. *Would Afghan leaders stand with us against the insurgency? Would they come out publicly in support of the Kabul-based government?* Too often, the response that came back was a version of, *How can I lend you my support when in eighteen months you will begin to leave? Your own president has said so. The Taliban shadow governor for my province, who lives down the road—he is not leaving in eighteen months.*

There were, of course, many reasons why we lost the war. However, as I tried to figure out how to answer my son, it occurred to me that of the many reasons we failed in Afghanistan, chief among them was that we never understood what winning meant. It wouldn't have mattered what year I left—from 2001 to 2021—because in any year we couldn't agree on what victory even looked like. And so we lost.

What does it mean to win a war? That depends on the stories we tell ourselves about war. When I was in high school, I first read the *Iliad.* The translation my teacher handed out had a single photograph on the cover: American GIs on D-Day storming out of a landing craft onto Omaha Beach. The subtext of this pairing wasn't obvious to me as a teenager. The rage of Achilles, the death of Hector and all those Greeks in their "black-hulled ships," seemed to have little to do with the Second World War. However, after fighting in two wars of my own, that image came to resonate in a new way, particularly as I tried to explain to my son what it meant to win or lose a

war. If the *Iliad* served as an urtext for ancient Greek wars (Alexander the Great is said to have slept with a copy beneath his pillow while on campaign), then the Second World War has served a similar function in our society, framing our expectations of war, becoming our American *Iliad*. We still expect to be the good guys; we expect there to be a beginning, a middle, and an end; and we expect that the war is over when the troops come home. But that final expectation—that a war is over only when all the troops come home—has never really held true, not in the Second World War and not today.

In Afghanistan there's something to be learned from Iraq: with Iraq, the great strategic blunder of the Bush administration was to *put* the troops in, while the great strategic blunder of the Obama administration was to *pull* the troops out. Both missteps created power vacuums. The first saw the flourishing of al-Qaeda in Iraq; the second gave birth to that group's successor, ISIS.

If insanity is doing the same thing over and over again and expecting a different outcome, in Afghanistan the Biden administration has adopted an insane policy, setting itself up for a repeat of Obama's experience in Iraq with what has proven to be a debacle of a withdrawal. Obama's decision to leave Iraq—like his decision to surge in Afghanistan while simultaneously announcing the date of his withdrawal— was another hedge. In the lead-up to the 2012 election, he needed to deliver on his 2008 campaign promise to end the war in Iraq. When on December 18, 2011, the last US troops crossed the border into Kuwait, Obama only needed conditions inside Iraq to remain stable for the eleven months between the withdrawal and his reelection; this was the decent interval he was gambling on, and he got it. On the stump in 2012, this allowed him to claim to have ended the war. If the Iraqi government and military collapsed after Election Day (as they did in the summer of 2014, when an Islamic State blitzkrieg advanced to within sixteen miles of Baghdad), it would prove beside the point politically.

Like Obama, the Biden administration seems to have made a similar hedge, gambling its Afghanistan policy on a decent interval between the withdrawal of US forces and the collapse of the Afghan government. A decent interval allows a degree of plausible deniability, or, as my son put it, the ability for us to say, "When we left, we were winning the war."

Although we weren't winning the war, the Afghan government had fought the Taliban to a stalemate when President Biden announced his withdrawal on April 13, 2021. On that day, according to the *Long War Journal*, of the 400 districts in Afghanistan, the Taliban could claim control of 77, the government could claim control of 129, and the reciprocal 194 remained contested in some way, while of Afghanistan's 33 provinces, the Taliban could claim control of none. They could also claim control of no major cities. For the Afghan government, this wasn't winning. But it wasn't quite losing either.

The American public has become conditioned to believe that wars only end when all the troops return home. Which speaks again to the *Iliad*, to the importance of the narratives we apply to our wars, and to our long-held misconceptions about homecomings. We currently have around 2,500 troops in Iraq, another 1,000 in Syria. Neither of those countries is at peace; our troops there continue to draw "imminent danger pay." Yet a month after the withdrawal from Afghanistan, in a speech at the United Nations, President Biden will say, "For the first time in twenty years the United States is not at war."

But what qualifies as a war? Clearly, it's not the deployment of US forces abroad. Few would argue that our enduring deployments in Western Europe or South Korea mean we are at war in these places. It is likely the combination of having US forces deployed abroad and those forces fighting and dying at a certain rate. If so, then what about our current commitments in countries like Iraq and Syria (to say nothing of places like Niger, or the Horn of Africa), where US combat deaths have held steady with recent combat deaths in Afghanistan. If we considered ourselves at war in Afghanistan, then we should consider ourselves at war in these places too. But we don't.

Unlike Afghanistan, we've been able to rationalize keeping troops in those countries by not categorizing ourselves as at war in them. President Biden has certainly ended the war in Afghanistan on more stringent conditions than those wars the United States has "ended" or not even acknowledged in other places. Those stringent conditions—specifically, the departure of all US troops by August 31—have led me back to my room for another night of coordinating evacuations.

Down the hallway, our children sleep. My phone continues to ping with updates. As my wife rests beside me in the bed, she whispers, "How's it going?" right as the message *Paused at the gate. Call in clearance* arrives.

I tell her that I'm not sure. I watch my phone:

Matt: At the wire.

Nick: copy.

Matt: CTPT soldiers radioing. We need you to call them now.

Nick: copy.

Matt: They don't want to let us in.

Ian: I'm calling my POCs.

Matt (addressing other vehicles in the convoy): Windows up.

Ian: On now. My POC at Team Cotton is calling his POC at airfield.

My wife asks whether they're opening the gate. "Not yet," I say. She's lying on her side, a segment of her face illuminated by the glow of my phone. "This is so unfair," she says. "You all shouldn't be the ones to have to do this. What if you can't get them out? Who is going to have to tell all those people that they're going to be left behind?" She throws an arm across my chest, not like she's hugging me, but more like how you'd restrain someone to protect them, as you would if they were about to step off the sidewalk into oncoming traffic. I met my wife after I left the war, and I know that she can feel it reasserting its hold over me because I can feel it myself.

In a jokey tone, I quote Michael Corleone in *The Godfather, Part III*: "Just when I thought I was out, they pull me back in." She doesn't laugh. Instead, she pulls me more tightly toward her. What I feel her trying to restrain me from, physically, is a moral injury, the one that Nick and I had been discussing before when we surmised how eventually one of these groups isn't going to be able to make it to the airport. People are going to be left behind. Because our government has no effective process to help our former allies, it is going to fall to us to say, *I'm sorry, but there's nothing more we can do to help you.*

When I was a boy, I was fascinated with the military. When I was six and seven, I used to pore over a well-worn illustrated history of the Vietnam War. I studied the photos on its pages for hours, the major American conflict of my parents' generation looming large in my young mind. As a Marine and, later, as a veteran, I met many men who'd fought in Vietnam. I admired them. And yet I sometimes felt they viewed my generation of all-volunteer veterans with skepticism, as if there must be something defective in us for freely choosing to return to war again and again. I confess I also thought the Vietnam guys were generally more bitter, that maybe they'd been more naive when they went to "their war," carrying more illusions into it, and so they wound up proportionately more disillusioned at its end.

This past week teaches me that I was wrong.

The difference between the Vietnam vets and my generation was far simpler: they had seen their war's last act. The skepticism I often encountered in their eyes, or the edge I detected when we talked about our respective experiences, wasn't disillusionment; it was pity, for me. They knew my war hadn't ended. They knew what was coming: betrayal. Of our allies, of our values, and of every American who was asked by this country to make promises to the Afghans only to end up like this, scrapping together an evacuation.

Eventually, my wife says, "I'm worried about how this is going to weigh on you all." Before I can answer her, my phone pings. It's Ian: *We're not getting an answer at the airfield, still calling.* Nick suggests we ask for Commander W., who had helped us through the gate the night before. Another couple of minutes pass; then Matt, who is at the gate, replies: *Commander W. left for America.*

SCENE V

Outskirts east of Shewan, 2008

Momez was dead and we were doing the math. The Taliban had shot out at least one tire on every vehicle. Most were leaking fluid. Many wouldn't start. We needed to salvage the tires and the parts off the most heavily damaged trucks and put them on the least damaged trucks. This would, we hoped, leave us with enough vehicles running so we could tow our damaged trucks back to base. But we also hoped to have enough vehicles to drive back into Shewan and recover Momez's body.

While half of us continued to swap sporadic gunfire with the Taliban, the other half formed into pit crews, breaking down our Humvees and swapping out parts. Tubes sat in the turret of my Humvee, his hastily bandaged hands clutching two radios as he called in successive sections of F-15s, F-18s, and B-1 bombers. They came in low over

Shewan, afterburners screaming. This kept the Taliban away from the one vehicle we'd left behind in the kill zone, the one that contained Momez's body. The only break Tubes took from coordinating with the pilots was to coordinate a helicopter medevac. A pair of Black Hawks landed in a cloud of dust as we loaded a half dozen of our wounded. With his burns, Tubes should've been on those Black Hawks. But Momez's body should've been on them too. And so Tubes wouldn't leave.

Momez's truck had been in the back of the convoy but in front of Tubes's truck. Momez was, when I last saw him, restacking the unused ammunition we'd brought to reinforce our sister team. There was so much extra ammunition that he was sitting on crates of it in the truck's bed as we pulled through Shewan. When the RPG hit Momez's truck, it had broken both his legs. When Tubes pulled up, he could see Momez struggling to free himself from the Humvee as the flames engulfed him. Those flames had also begun to cook off the crates of ammunition. Our own machine gun rounds exploded in every direction. Tubes went after Momez anyway.

When I saw Tubes, all he'd said was, "I couldn't get close enough." The burns on his arms and face, the way he was still coughing from smoke inhalation, and the vacant tone in his voice—as if he'd already begun the psychological coping process of disassociating himself from what he'd seen—it all spelled out in an instant the desperate but unsuccessful attempt he'd made to save Momez.

Tubes was still coordinating aircraft from the turret of my Humvee when Willy and Super Dave found me by its hood. Willy carried a green waterproof notebook, which he folded open and placed in front of me. Written across two sheets of paper was a new load-out plan for our convoy, to include those vehicles that would be driven and those that would be towed, as well as who would ride where. When I asked how many vehicles we'd have left over to go back into Shewan with and recover Momez, he answered, "Two. Every other vehicle is towing another." What he didn't say, but what was obvious, was that if the Taliban managed to disable either of those vehicles, we'd have to fight our way out of Shewan with one vehicle towing another, a scenario that would certainly turn into two disabled vehicles, leaving those of us who'd gone to get Momez stranded inside the town. I asked Willy what he thought. He shrugged, saying, "It's your call, sir. I do think that someone's going to get hurt—maybe killed—if we go in there. I can't see it any other way. So we should expect that."

I asked the same of Super Dave, who said, "You're the mission commander. We'll do whatever you want." But Dave and I were peers, and the only reason I was the mission commander today was because it was my turn. He'd be the mission commander the next time we went out, and as a member of the special forces detachment, Momez was Super Dave's soldier, so I pushed him a little harder for his opinion. He glanced down at the ground and said, "Momez is dead. Do I think he'd want one of us to get killed or even hurt trying to get his body? No, I don't think he'd want that. Does it matter that we get out his body? Of course it does. It'll matter to his family."

Dave wouldn't say more. He understood only one person could hold command at a time. If he'd given me his recommendation and I'd done the opposite, that schism would have a negative effect on the mission. All too often, rhetoric around war is portrayed as right versus wrong, good versus evil, black versus white, but if war has a color, it's gray. However, the decision I had to make did have a very clear rhetorical solution: *You never leave a man behind.* This is what we're taught in training, and it's a truism that isn't simply an invention of the modern US military. It's rooted in the oldest stories society tells about war, back to the Trojans and the Greeks, back to King Priam sneaking into the camp of Achilles in the dead of night to plead for the body of his slain son Hector. ("I have endured what no mortal ever endured. I have kissed the hands of the man who slaughtered my children.") The expectation to endure is clear. We don't leave our dead with the enemy.

But war—as opposed to the rhetoric applied to war—is filled with contradictions. Ostensibly, we fight wars to preserve one form of civilization over another. Fundamental to any civilization is the rule not to kill. Yet in war we suspend that rule. We engage in state-sanctioned slaughter to protect the civilized structures that prevent slaughter. And so contradiction is baked into war, which is why black-and-white platitudes fail in situations whose real hue is a muddled gray. Trying to reconcile that gray is also why madness and war so frequently attend each other. How many men with their whole lives ahead should sacrifice themselves for the body of one who is already dead? One? Six? Twelve? Once again, it seems our situation comes down to a matter of math. In my wars, I have taken life. But I have saved life too. Does one balance out the other? And what of those who have neither taken nor saved a life? What is the mathematics of their morality versus my own? A person could ponder it for a lifetime.

I reached through the window of my Humvee and Redbone passed me the handset. The satellite radio was tuned to the frequency of the special operations task force in Bagram. While I updated the watch officer on our situation, I couldn't help but notice how not only Redbone but also Willy, Super Dave, and Tubes eavesdropped on the conversation. After passing along an updated status report—personnel, equipment, ammunition—I provided my assessment of the situation. If we attempted to reenter Shewan with the small force available to us, we'd likely sustain further casualties and could potentially find ourselves in a situation where we were cut off. I then requested that the task force reinforce us before we attempted a recovery mission. The request had hardly left my mouth when the major I worked for came up on the net: "Negative. No such reinforcements are available. You need to begin the recovery immediately."

All pretense of eavesdropping vanished. Everyone was now actively listening to our conversation. The radio hissed as the major's last transmission seemed to hang in the air. Those congregated around the Humvee were all staring at me. Much depended on my response. People have, at times, asked me whether I regret having fought in the wars in Iraq and Afghanistan given their outcomes. When trying to answer that, I've often come back to this moment and perhaps a dozen others like it; that's only a dozen such moments over the eight years I spent at war. But they were moments when I knew the decision I had to make was of real consequence—life-and-death consequence. I don't presume to know if in every instance I made the exact right decision, but I know it was worth it to me to be there to make that decision. There are many things in war that I've since regretted or felt unclear about. Having been present at these moments is not one of them.

However, what followed is something that I've always felt unclear about.

I answered the major by reiterating our tenuous situation in terms of equipment and personnel. But before I could finish, he interrupted, "Your situation is understood. I say again: begin recovery efforts *immediately.*"

The special operations task force in Bagram wasn't primarily made up of Marines but of special forces soldiers, like Super Dave, who himself had a close relationship with the special forces colonel our major worked for. Super Dave stepped around the back of my truck and called the colonel on an Iridium satellite phone while I monitored the radio. When Dave returned a moment later, he said, "We need to remain ready to go, but they're going to look into contingency plans."

The words had no sooner left Super Dave's mouth than the major came back up on the radio. He parroted the same message.

It was late afternoon. The light coming out of the west and sweeping the town was golden. The sun, at this angle, was now in our eyes. It refracted through the smoke of the fires that still burned in Shewan, to include the one that had consumed Momez's Humvee, and the light at this angle cast the day's destruction in harsher relief. Every plume of smoke became visible. The shadows of newly broken buildings cast their jagged patterns through the town. The sporadic gunfire from the outskirts ebbed. We waited like this, in the near silence, for another twenty minutes or so.

The major came back up on the radio. Our sister team—the one we'd reinforced—had made it back to their base. They could refuel, rearm, and be back in Shewan at full strength tonight to recover Momez's body. Our special operations task force had not only prioritized aircraft to support their recovery effort but had also arranged for aircraft to remain continuously overhead lest the Taliban try to snatch

Momez's body. Tubes would stay with us and coordinate the aircraft from the ground, while our entire force would remain in the area in case our sister team needed reinforcement. Our convoy would hold up in a nearby outpost, one manned by a few dozen army infantrymen where the Ring Road branched into the access road that had taken us to Shewan.

Willy had been listening as I coordinated the last of these details with the major. When I set the radio handset aside, whatever expression I was wearing caused Willy to put his hand on my shoulder and say, "This was the right call, skipper. You should feel good about that." What Willy could see was that I didn't feel "right" or "good" about any of it. Tonight, our sister team would go into Shewan to get Momez. One of two things would happen. They would either (a) recover Momez without incident, finishing a job we should've finished ourselves, or (b) meet significant resistance in Shewan, taking casualties of their own to finish the job that we couldn't. Either way, as our convoy limped toward the Ring Road and the outpost where we'd pause for the night, a measure of guilt settled its weight on me. The only way I could have avoided that weight would have been to successfully return to Shewan—understrength and underequipped—and get Momez's body out.

Maybe that's what I should've done.

I'll never know.

We pulled into the outpost after dark. The Taliban had shot up Tubes's vehicle so badly that the auxiliary power running its radios no longer worked, and so he drove with me instead, coordinating aircraft from the back seat. The soldiers at the outpost lived hard, sleeping on foam mats in either sandbagged fighting positions or the slit trenches they'd cut into the rocky desert. When our convoy arrived, they emerged from their positions, curiously welcoming us. They gawked like stargazers as they pointed out the constellations of bullet holes and fragmentation gouges that pocked our vehicles. Their leader, a long-limbed lieutenant with a coating of stubble across his cheeks, gave a low whistle. "Lookee here," he said with a singsong southern drawl as he shook his head in wonder. "Your fight up the road sounded bad. Not this bad, though. You're welcome to stay long as you like. We can't offer you much. Resupply hasn't been through in a week." He gestured to a pallet of bottled water and a few leftover cases of MREs.

Willy, who was always good at making friends, scrounged up some Gatorade powder from our trucks. He helped the thirsty grunts mix up a five-gallon jug's worth. I was sitting up on the roof of my Humvee with Tubes when he came by, offering us each a canteen-cupful, which we took. It reddened our mouths as we waited for our sister team to begin their sprint into the center of Shewan. Tubes and I weren't alone. Every truck with a radio had a small cluster of us listening and drinking red Gatorade.

Then, when Willy left, Tubes apologized to me.

I was surprised. "What are you sorry for?"

We were facing toward the west. The sun had long since set, and there was nothing but darkness in that direction. It took Tubes a minute to choose his words, but when he did, he explained, "I thought I could get him out, but I couldn't. The fire was too intense. But if I had gotten him out, then we wouldn't be in this mess. If the guys doing the recovery get hurt tonight, that'll be on me."

"No, it won't," I said, cutting him off. But of course, the logic of Tubes's guilt mirrored the logic of my own. He wasn't thinking about what, in fact, *could've* happened—because he *couldn't* have done more; rather, he was thinking of what *should've* happened—Momez *shouldn't* have died. But that was outside his control.

I said this to him.

He looked back as though he wasn't quite convinced. He simply said, "I don't know," and I wondered then—and have wondered since—who absolves us of such regrets. If Tubes's burns weren't enough to convince him that he'd done everything in his power to save Momez, then what would convince him? Or was it even possible to convince him? To have lived when others have died means to question why. That question has few satisfying answers. Better not to ask it; that is, if you can resist its allure, which I also said to Tubes as we sat there. What I said specifically was, "It is what it is." Which was a caution, a way of saying that the question he was asking turns survival itself into a dilemma, one that traps you between guilt and death.

Our sister team came up on the radio. They had begun their movement into Shewan. Disciplined and professional, their curt radio transmissions marked their progress as they passed into town, calling out checkpoints. When they arrived at Momez's charred vehicle they remained equally cool, offering up a sharp "At the objective." Tubes and I watched the drone's live feed on his tablet as their grainy silhouettes fanned out around the vehicle. What quickly followed was "Objective secure." Then another few minutes passed. Once they recovered Momez, they would need to call in his kill number. Each of us had one. It was the first two letters of your last name and then the last four of your social security number. When calling in medevacs we used kill numbers instead of names so that everyone on the net wouldn't immediately be able to identify the casualty. Medevacs are called in with three priority levels. The highest is *urgent*, which is for "loss of life or limb." The next is *priority*, "patient's condition is stable but requires care." The last is *routine*, "personnel's condition is not expected to worsen significantly."

The dead are classified *routine*.

Our sister team calls out Momez's kill number—"November, Uniform . . ."—as they formally request one routine medevac. With that done, they announce that they're returning to base, as well as their status: "Mission complete."

SCENE VI

A hotel room, Venice, at night

The Unnamed Gate will remain closed. Ian's contact in Senator Cotton's office can't convince the CIA to open it. In the chat, Nick wonders whether the convoy should simply return to the Serena Hotel and try again tomorrow night. Matt puts this question to the 145 Afghans riding the buses. He relays their response to us over the chat: *That's a hard no.*

If the perimeter of HKIA were a clockface, the Unnamed Gate would be located at the twelve o'clock position. Our convoy remains pulled off on the shoulder of the road here. Rumors are that the traffic around the North Gate, which is at the two o'clock position, is relatively light.

Earlier that day, I'd swapped emails with the lieutenant colonel in command of the Marines at the North Gate. His name is Chris Richardella. His battalion—the 1st Battalion of the 8th Marine Regiment,

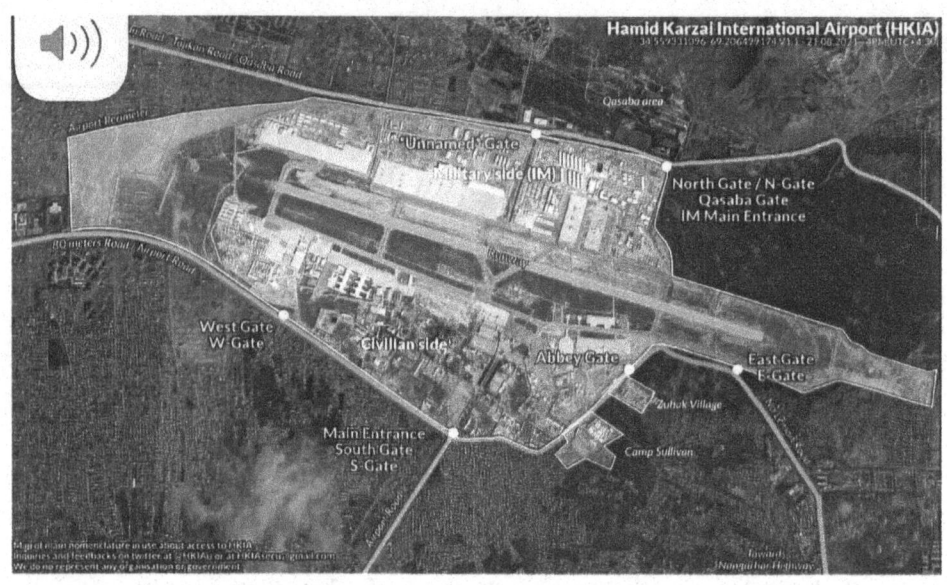

said "one-eight" in Marine speak—is my old infantry battalion, the one I fought in as a twenty-four-year-old platoon commander in Fallujah. They're known as the "Beirut Battalion" because nearly forty years before, on October 23, 1983, Marines from 1/8 were guarding the airport in Beirut when Hezbollah detonated a pair of truck bombs, killing 241 Americans. Given 1/8's legacy, its deployment to HKIA only adds to the myriad minor subplots in the drama unfolding at the airport.

One of those minor subplots is that Chris Richardella, or "Rich" as he's called, is an old friend. We attended our Marine Corps officer training together in Quantico nearly two decades ago. That the end of a war would serve as an overdue reunion for those who participated in that war is an irony of this evacuation. Sitting up in my hotel room bed, with my cell phone plugged into the wall, I'm cursing myself for not having kept in better touch with Rich over the years. The cell phone number I have for him is old, and he's not picking up as our buses head toward the North Gate.

As I'm scrambling through my contacts, Nick, Ian, and everyone else on the chat is doing the same. We're all searching for someone—anyone, really—who might be able to help us open one of these gates. The team aboard the convoy is getting impatient, posting *Find us an open gate* on the chat.

It is getting close to morning. I can't get through to Rich. Our convoy is now stalled outside the North Gate. Nick calls me directly. The Rockefeller Foundation, which has partially funded one of our charter flights, has connections to the Brookings Institution, whose president, John Allen, is the former commanding general of US Central Command. "We're trying to reach him," Nick explains.

Whatever frustration or despair I'd felt a moment before vanishes.

I know General Allen ... sort of. More than a year ago, we'd sat at the same table at a dinner in Washington, D.C. He'd graciously invited me to visit him at his office. A month later, we'd spent a pleasant afternoon sipping coffee and reminiscing about our wars. I put Nick on speaker while I scroll through my contacts. And there it is: General Allen's cell phone number.

I call.

"Elliot, good to hear from you," he says, and then, without missing a beat, adds, "So, it sounds like we've got ourselves a bit of a situation." A representative from the Rockefeller Foundation has already contacted him, so he's somewhat read into our problem at the airport. He offers to call his former colleagues at Central Command and, hopefully, get them to open a gate for our convoy. We agree that I'll text him the name and phone number for the convoy point of contact (which is Matt) and that he'll then pass that along to the Centcom J-3, the officer in charge of operations. I also put him directly in touch with Nick.

After I hang up, my wife rolls over. Sleepily, she asks, "Who was that?"

"General Allen."

"Centcom General Allen?"

"Yeah," I say, and begin texting the broader group with an update. "He's going to call some of his old colleagues to get them to open the gate for us."

"That's so messed up," she says.

"What's messed up? He said he'll help."

"He shouldn't have to help. It shouldn't come down to General Allen, or to you, or Nick, or Ian. Can you not see that?" She's exasperated. Her tone is such that it's as though we're in an intervention, one where she's trying to make me see the nature of an abusive relationship I've been trapped inside. "It's just poignant," she says. "To see all of you trying to finish this, with so little help. It's a total collapse." She pushes her body close to mine.

Collapse is a good word. The past couple of weeks have been not only a collapse of our country's competence as we've unconditionally lost a twenty-year war, but also a collapse of time, space, and hierarchy.

Time has collapsed, as those of us who fought in Afghanistan years ago have found ourselves thrown back into that conflict with an intensity as though we'd never left.

Space has collapsed, as those of us coordinating these evacuations are spread across the world in places as far-flung as France (Nick), Virginia (Ian), and Italy (me), to say nothing of those on the buses in Kabul, like Matt.

And hierarchy has collapsed, as from the president of the United States on down, we are all subject to the vicissitudes of this catastrophic withdrawal.

An hour passes. Then two. It is morning now.

The Centcom J-3 instructs our convoy to head to the South Gate, which is located at the six o'clock position along the airport's perimeter. Crowds at the South Gate can be bad. Still, the J-3 insists this is the only way into the airport. Also, our entrance will have to be negotiated with the Taliban, which maintains its own checkpoint outside the gate. Matt drives ahead to scout out conditions. Thirty minutes later, he returns with this message: *Traffic is bad but situation at roundabout and gate is OK, you gotta go through and loop into that lane that leads into the airport. Not sure if the Talibs will let you through though, got whacked upside the head for asking.*

There's chatter among the others in the buses: *Shit you ok? . . .* followed by, *I think let's just roll up. No other choice.*

They go.

We monitor the convoy's progress in the chat. The cadence of the updates is familiar. Bus 3: *Lead vehicle needs to slow up.* Bus 1: *We're waiting.* Bus 3: *Gotcha.* Bus 1: *Rolling.* Each of these minor communications seems to build toward a climax; that climax is, of course, the success or failure of the mission, whether our convoy will make it through the South Gate.

Bus 2: How's it look?

Bus 1: Stuck in traffic before airport roundabout now.

Nick is coordinating with Centcom. He posts, *They will let you in. Asking for ETA?*

Bus 1: 5 min

Nick: [From Centcom] "Keep pushing. Don't divert."

Bus 2: Pushing.

Bus 1: U-turn into airport lane now

Nick: Please advise when convoy is at gate. They will assist.

Bus 3: 2 min

Bus 2: We are spread out. Cars got between.

(Those two minutes pass.)

Bus 2: Gotta get through traffic and Taliban. They are spraying the crowd with fire hoses.

(Another two minutes pass.)

Bus 1: Convoy is at gate

Nick: Copy

Bus 1: Talibs saying they need green light from inside airport

Nick: Copy and passed on

Bus 2: Lead bus stuck at the gate. Crowds are trying to enter bus.

Nick: Copy

Bus 1: Has to happen now boys

Nick: passed on

Bus 1: K moving

Nick: all buses?

Bus 1: Only first for now. Who has the list?

(The manifest is reposted in the chat, 145 people in four buses.)

Bus 2: Second bus not moving.

Bus 1: They want the list coming from the inside. From the Americans, I guess.

Bus 2: Humvee blocking us. A Talib Humvee is blocking the way. Nick can you pass up the list?

Nick: More info from the ground please. Allen is asking.

Bus 1: They're not letting us in for now

Bus 2: We are stuck. Crowds around trying to get in buses. We need to pass the Talib checkpoint.

Matt: On my way

Bus 1: Who has the printed list? Lots of shooting. They won't let us in.

Nick: Copy

Bus 1: Quick please it's chaos. Nick can the US pass word from inside?

Nick: Asking. Allen speaking to Centcom in real time, doing everything he can.

Matt: On foot in the roundabout, got eyes on the convoy

Bus 1: The talibs need the list and the license plates of the buses and it has to come from the americans

Matt: I'm beside first bus

Bus 1: They're sending us back. It has to come from americans inside.

Nick: Allen is interceding. "Centcom acknowledged all info passed to coordination cell. They understand the urgency."

Bus 1: Not gonna happen guys.

Bus 2: We're blocked from behind.

Bus 1: Backing up

Bus 3: Are bus 1 and 2 out of line? Are we following?

Nick: Centcom does not promise immediate resolution. If you can leave, I would leave.

Bus 2: Guys?

Matt: Regroup by the white wedding hall. Southbound road.

Bus 2: Aborting

Bus 1: Yeah lets fall back to serena

Nick: Any injuries?

Bus 2: None

Bus 1: All good

Bus 3: Only dignity

Matt: I will wait for last bus. Rest of you go back.

From start to finish, this attempt on the South Gate takes a little over an hour.

No one has slept much over the past two days. My wife is brushing her teeth in the bathroom when we finally abort. The day ahead, in which we'll sightsee with our children, is so psychically disconnected from the night I've spent monitoring events in Kabul that I struggle to understand which is real—last night, or today—and conclude that perhaps neither is real, that I am neither here nor there, that I am psychically nowhere.

Then my phone pings with yet another text, though this one isn't from our aborted convoy. It's from Rich. He's at the North Gate. If our convoy can get there, the Marines from 1-8 will let them into the airport. I post this in the chat.

Matt responds, *Traffic is a problem even at night. My guess is we will have to stop several hundred meters off. I don't think we can bring four buses to that gate during the day, based on my previous visits, even if we do have access.*

I respond, *Understood.*

Matt adds, *My vote is to go back to the Serena.*

Forty minutes later, when the last of the buses arrives at the Serena Hotel, I am in the restaurant of my hotel alone sipping coffee. Our tour guide is in the lobby. Everyone is waiting on me. It's time to begin the day.

ACT III

THE NORTH GATE

My original instinct was to pull out—and, historically, I like following my instincts.

—PRESIDENT DONALD TRUMP
ARLINGTON NATIONAL CEMETERY
AUGUST 21, 2017

SCENE I

Lobby of the Essex House, New York, 2016

"And what name is the room under again, sir?"

"Ackerman," I say. "Nate Ackerman."

The receptionist clacks furiously on his keyboard, typing out a great deal more than twelve letters. My brother is staying in the hotel. I've brought my two children over. We're supposed to meet him in the lobby and then head to dinner nearby. He's late and not answering his cell phone, so I think to try the hotel phone but don't know his room number. My children, who are four and six years old, tug impatiently at my pant legs. They're bored. They begin to swat at each other. I shush them and press them more closely to my side. The receptionist says, "I'm not seeing him. Can you spell the name for me?"

"Ackerman," I repeat, then enunciate each letter: "A-C-K-E-R-M-A-N."

Then behind me I hear, "Elliot Ackerman?"

When I turn around, I'm met by a bearded man with a shaved-bald head. Professorially dressed, he's wearing a Harris Tweed sports coat with suede elbow patches. In one hand he carries his luggage, a monogrammed calfskin weekender. In the other hand he carries an umbrella; its handle appears to be some type of polished horn. He tucks the umbrella under his left arm and extends his right hand toward me. "Jesus," he says. "It's been a long time."

His name is Dutch; to be exact, it's been a little more than five years since he and I last saw each other in Afghanistan. A former Marine aviator, Dutch had an accomplished career as a helicopter pilot before giving up the cockpit for a career as a paramilitary case officer. He had flown everything from medevac missions in Fallujah to the president of the United States. When we worked together at the CIA, Dutch was our air officer. Our CTPT relied on him to coordinate everything from close air support to surveillance flights to parachute resupplies. A born eccentric, Dutch existed at the Venn diagram intersection of Allen Dulles's Cold War CIA and the ensemble cast of a Wes Anderson film. He maintained an exquisite collection of pipes, to include several by Dunhill that he would generously share. On days-long cross-country patrols, I soon took to smoking with Dutch in our truck, our night-vision goggles shielding our eyes, our pipes planted in our mouths and chimneying smoke, while Ali—who was my interpreter in those days—sat in the back, his head lolling out the window sucking at the fresh air. Dutch wore his eccentricity like a suit of armor that insulated him from the harsher realities of our war. He went so far as to found the Shkin Gun, Pipe, and Kennel Club, or what he insisted on referring to as the SGPKC. To become a member, you had to have a gun (which we all did), smoke a pipe (which few of us did), and put out food for the feral dogs we'd adopted (which we all did)—so membership really came down to whether you smoked a pipe. He even had T-shirts made up.

I've missed him.

When I ask what he's doing in the city, he explains, "I just got back from a work trip. The wife and I thought we'd take a weekend away."

I don't ask him where the work trip was. The security clearances I once held, I no longer do, and I don't want to put him in an awkward position by asking where he's been. And so I introduce him to my children instead. They each step forward, say their name, and shake his hand. They look Dutch in the eye as I've done my best to teach them. Then their uncle appears in the lobby. Their composure vanishes as they run over to greet him. My mathematician brother—who is also a beloved eccentric—apologizes for being late. He'd dozed off in his room. We're headed to dinner, and so is Dutch. But he and I agree to meet up in the Essex House bar for a drink at the end of the night, to catch up.

In addition to the work Dutch and I did together on patrols for the CTPT, we also worked together in the gathering of intelligence around Shkin. We each managed a stable of assets, from low-level informants to recruited agents. Certain cases we managed together, one of which was a Waziri tribesman we'd nicknamed "Chuckles," given a nervous tic of his. When he got anxious, he'd hiccup with laughter. And frequently at inexplicable moments. Chuckles lived in Pakistan, though he often crossed the porous border into Afghanistan to meet with us. His particular area of expertise, or utility, was what we termed "BDAs," battle damage assessments. These BDAs typically occurred after predator strikes inside Pakistan's tribal areas, in which we would need to confirm whether we had killed our target.

My first day as a paramilitary case officer came about a year before I met Chuckles. I spent it at CIA headquarters filling out paperwork: a health care plan, a Roth IRA, a parking pass application, a stipend for childcare. This was in the summer of 2009, and I'd come to the CIA after my time in Marine Corps special operations. Having spent my entire adult life working for the federal government, I'd expected the paper chase, but mixed in with the forms, one stood out—Executive Order 12333, which includes this clause: "No person employed by or acting on behalf of the United States Government shall engage in, or conspire to engage in, assassination."

This seemed straightforward enough. Silenced pistols and cyanide-laced cocktails were for the movies; they weren't the stuff of real intelligence work. So I signed the order. I was giving more thought to whether a rookie like me could land a decent parking spot at the agency's headquarters in Northern Virginia. A few months later, I began my initial deployment. As a paramilitary case officer, I trained and operated alongside the CTPT, but I also worked alongside non-paramilitary case officers. Our combined work space was always a windowless vault. My colleagues stayed indoors, behind banks of computers, planning out drone strikes. The toll of the months they'd been deployed showed in their sallow complexions. Dossier upon dossier cluttered their desktops—Taliban senior leaders, al-Qaeda operatives, each one targeted for killing. For assassination.

Granted, lawyers working for multiple presidential administrations had drawn up semantic arguments carefully delineating the difference between a targeted killing and an assassination. But when the picture of the person you were trying to kill sat on your desk, when you watched the predator strikes light up the night sky just across the border, and then when you took that same picture and moved it into a file for archiving, it sure felt like an assassination.

The discomfort of my colleagues, where it existed, didn't stem from the act itself. The dossiers were filled with details about Taliban commanders and al-Qaeda operatives—people we had identified as valid targets, who were known to have killed our comrades in Afghanistan, or to have ambitions to launch attacks in the United States or Western Europe. The discomfort existed because it felt like we were doing something, on a large scale, that we'd sworn not to. Most of us felt as though we were violating Executive Order 12333. Everybody knew what was happening—senior intelligence officials, general officers, the administration, even the American people, who ostensibly would not tolerate assassinations carried out in their name.

In the United States, we veiled these assassination programs behind the highest levels of classification. In Afghanistan and Pakistan—to say nothing of countries from Syria to Yemen to Somalia—these assassination programs became a part of daily life. They were no secret to the residents of these countries, while to us, in our country, these campaigns became a secret we kept from ourselves.

Which brings us back to Chuckles. He arrived at the gate to our firebase on the morning after a predator strike in Wana, a hamlet across the border in Pakistan. After being searched, he was escorted to a meeting room, which was little more than a plywood hut with a sofa and coffee table flanked by two plastic chairs. Dutch and I sat in the plastic chairs. Chuckles sat on the deep pleather sofa, which threatened to swallow his slight frame.

"What have you got for us?" asked Dutch.

A bowl of M&M's sat on the table. Chuckles had already taken a palmful, which seemed to be his breakfast. He ate them one at a time as he spoke. "Yesterday afternoon, there was an explosion not far from the Wana bazaar."

He paused, as if for dramatic effect. He volleyed his gaze between me and Dutch, blinking repeatedly. His long, dark, almost feminine eyelashes fluttered as he tried to get a read on us. "Really?" I said. "Was anyone hurt in the explosion?"

"Yes," he answered cautiously. "Four Talibs were killed." He popped a couple more M&M's into his mouth. His shoulders hiccupped as he began to laugh.

Yesterday's strike had taken out a single vehicle, so four dead Talibs made sense. I asked, "Do you know who they were?"

He shook his head. "I could maybe find out."

I glanced at Dutch. Historically, Chuckles didn't respond well to complex follow-on taskings. Asking him to find out would likely prove more hassle than it was worth. Furthermore, the strike had targeted a senior Taliban commander named Nazir. Neither Dutch nor I wanted Chuckles to know about our interest in Nazir or that we'd nearly pinpointed his location. Dutch chimed in, moving our debriefing in a slightly different direction: "Did you see the strike?"

"No," said Chuckles. "I only heard about it."

"Where?" I asked.

"In my cousin's shop," said Chuckles. "Some people had been nearby when the explosion happened, and they were talking about it."

"Who?" asked Dutch.

Chuckles stared at the ceiling as if reassembling the scene from memory. "At my cousin's shop was . . ." And he began to list a series of names, none of whom we recognized as being individuals of any intelligence value, though we dutifully copied down each name in our notes. Then, as Chuckles came to the end of this recounting, he added a final name: "And Commander Nazir, he was there too."

"Commander Nazir was at your cousin's shop?" I asked.

"Yes," said Chuckles. "He often comes there."

I glanced at Dutch. Chuckles, noting that glance, began to laugh again. He then stuffed a few more M&M's into his mouth.

"How often does he come?" Dutch asked.

Chuckles told us that Commander Nazir would typically arrive at his cousin's shop for tea and conversation once or twice a week in the afternoon. Dutch stood from his chair and sat on the sofa, so that he now flanked Chuckles. I did the same. Facing us was Dutch's computer. He had brought up a satellite map of Wana on its screen. "Could you show us where your cousin's shop is?"

Chuckles leaned forward. He stared into the computer as though looking over the side of a cliff. I explained that the orientation of the satellite image was from overhead. He blinked a couple of times, tucking his chin toward his chest like he was overcome by vertigo.

Dutch and I had seen this problem before. If a person wasn't familiar with reading maps or had never seen their home from the vantage point of a satellite, the overhead imagery could be difficult to comprehend and would require us to reorient their perspective and walk them through what they were seeing. Dutch, ever the aviator, took up this task. "Imagine you are like a bird—"

Chuckles interjected, "Like the hawk?"

"Yes, like the hawk," said Dutch, who even began flapping his arms like wings for effect. "You are flying over Wana. What you see in this image is what the hawk would see looking down from the sky. Do you understand?"

Chuckles gave an encouraging grin. He liked thinking of himself as a hawk. When his attention returned to the satellite imagery, he sat silently between us, blinking his eyes and kneading his stubbly chin. He still couldn't pinpoint the location of his cousin's shop.

Now I tried. "How about from the military base?" I pointed to one of the largest congregations of buildings on the map. "Can you tell us how you would walk to your cousin's shop from there?"

Chuckles laughed nervously. He didn't know the way.

"Or from here?" I said, pointing to an open field by one of the main roads. "From the sports grounds—how would you get to your cousin's shop from there?"

He took another handful of M&M's, as though if he ate enough of our candy, he might be able to see the world below the way we needed him to see it. With his mouth filled, he continued to stare vacantly at our map.

Clearly, this wasn't working. "Okay," I said, "why don't you pick a place that everyone knows and tell us how to get to your cousin's shop from there."

Chuckles glanced back at me. "A place that everyone knows?"

"Yes," added Dutch. "Pick a place that is familiar to you."

Chuckles knitted his eyebrows together. He inhaled a ponderous breath and then exhaled in an excited rush. He'd figured out the perfect place. "Commander Nazir's *house*!" he said. "I can show you how to get to my cousin's shop from Commander Nazir's *house*!"

I crossed my arms over my chest. Dutch shut his notebook.

We asked Chuckles if he would just show us where Commander Nazir lived.

Seven years pass. I've put my children to bed and made my way back to the bar of the Essex House; here, Dutch and I are telling the old stories, including that one. He reminds me that the raw intelligence we gleaned from Chuckles that day found its way into the president's daily briefing—the two of us had received a congratulatory cable from headquarters—and not for the first time, we laugh about how terrifying it is to imagine that a direct line could exist from Chuckles to the president of the United States. I then wonder aloud about whatever happened to Chuckles.

"Oh, he's still there," says Dutch.

"He is?"

"Yeah." Dutch takes a sip of his cocktail. "I probably saw him . . . I dunno, three or four weeks ago."

It's hard for me to get my mind around this. In the intervening years, Chuckles has become a totem within my memory more than a person. I ask what he's doing these days.

"Same shit," says Dutch. "BDAs mostly. He got in a bit of trouble a few years back, selling the same intel to different case officers. But he's still working for us. What else is he going to do?"

"So you were back in Afghanistan for this last trip?"

"Yeah," says Dutch. "I'm mostly in and out of there these days."

"I would've thought it had slowed down."

"Why would you think that?"

I unhinge my jaw to speak but realize I don't really know why I thought that. Perhaps, like with Chuckles, the war had come to exist so prominently in my memory that it was difficult to imagine that it still existed in the present.

Dutch explains that the drawdown of conventional forces from Afghanistan has led to an increasing reliance on clandestine forces. That burden, combined with the war against the Islamic State in Iraq and Syria, as well as commitments in Yemen, Somalia, and even Ukraine, keep him on the road more than half the year. Like a gourmand who's tried every dish on the menu only to discover he likes the house special the best, Dutch explains his enduring affinity for Afghanistan.

He glances at his watch. It's late, and his wife is upstairs waiting.

I tell him that it'd be good to see him again.

"It would," he says. "I'm headed back in a few weeks."

"Then maybe we could grab lunch one day around here?"

"No, sorry," he says. "I meant that I'm headed back to Afghanistan in a few weeks. Not *here*." Dutch has no idea when he'll next be in New York. We swap numbers nonetheless, and he promises that if he ever does make it back he'll call.

SCENE II

The Hotel Danieli, Venice

My wife's father was well into his fifties when she was born. He and her mother had a twenty-year age difference. Long before he had my wife, and long before he met her mother, he'd fought in the Second World War. He'd served in the OSS back then, in East Asia. He earned a Bronze Star for rescuing downed fliers from behind enemy lines. He spoke fluent French. In photos, he is debonair, with a pencil-thin mustache; he sits at a table with other OSS officers in front of a map, where they are no doubt planning one of these daring rescue missions. He returned home after the war and became a trial lawyer, one revered within his community. Stories are still told about his greatest cases and closing arguments. I wish I'd met him. People in my wife's family wish that I'd met him. He is most often compared to two people, both fictional characters: Atticus Finch and James Bond.

His favorite restaurant, in Venice, was on the rooftop of the Hotel Danieli. It overlooks the mouth of the Grand Canal. Months before—when the Afghan government still held Kabul—my wife had made a dinner reservation for us here. Neither of us has slept much the past few nights, and we've had full days with our children. We consider canceling our booking and staying in. Because the restaurant was her father's favorite, I ask my wife whether he would've kept the booking or stayed in. She says unequivocally that he would never think to miss a dinner at the Danieli.

We sit on the rooftop. The night is perfect, warm and clear. The view over the canal is spectacular. The Salute, with its domed basilica, sits diagonally across the water from us on the Punta della Dogana. Carved into its lit-up facade are four ornate statues of the four apostles turned saints: Matthew, Mark, Luke, and John. Each sits in a perch above the basilica's entrance. Looking across the water at the saints, I know my wife feels close to her father here, and we talk about him. His love of travel. His love of learning. "To follow knowledge like a sinking star" was a bit of Tennyson he quoted fondly. He loved his home, his family. But he was restless too.

My wife tells me—not for the first time—of some of the ways that I remind her of him. It is, of course, flattering to be so favorably compared to her father. Sitting on this rooftop, I imagine him here at around my age, launched into his second career, into his second life, with his beautiful wife beside him and this ancient and singular city spread below like a land he'd conquered in his youth.

His war was fought by the Greatest Generation. My war was fought primarily by the Millennial Generation. A Marine turned cop I once met, a veteran of the war in Afghanistan, told me that the reason he'd enlisted, in 2009 at age seventeen, was because of his reaction to 9/11 eight years before. When I pointed out that this seemed like a rather dramatic reaction for a nine-year-old to have had, he'd said, "There's a stigma around millennials, but people forget that millennials fought America's longest wars as volunteers."

I was born in 1980, which, depending on your definition, might make me a millennial, but I've never felt like one. I mentioned this once to another friend of mine, a former bomb technician who'd fought in Iraq. He's about my age. He said he'd never felt like a millennial either, so he'd come up with a different generational criterion: if you were old enough to have had an adult reaction to the September 11 attacks, you're not a millennial. By that criterion, I'm not a millennial after all. But neither is my friend, the Marine turned cop. At nine years old, he'd had a distinctly adult reaction: he'd decided to enlist, and eight years later he'd gone through with it, convincing his parents to sign an age waiver. Wars, which were once shared as generational touchstones, are no longer experienced the same way in America because of our all-volunteer military. In the past, did this make the return home less jarring? Perhaps so. I'd rather be part of a lost generation, I think, than be the lost part of a generation.

In 2017, in an effort to shape generational memory, Congress passed the Global War on Terrorism War Memorial Act, which authorized the construction of a monument on the National Mall. One of the bill's cosponsors was Representative Seth Moulton. Seth and I are contemporaries from the Marines, and not long after the bill's passage, he and I took a run past some of the potential sites for the memorial on the mall. We'd met in front of the Longworth House Office Building early on a muggy July morning. Seth had been wearing an old desert-brown Under Armour shirt from his Iraq days. We'd jogged west on the south side of the mall, skirting the vast lawn along with the other joggers as we progressed toward the Lincoln Memorial. When I asked him how he might design a memorial to our wars, he laughed, saying, "In another life I would've liked to have been an architect." I pressed him on the question. He was, after all, a cosponsor of the legislation. If this memorial came to be, it'd be in large part due to his efforts. Eventually, he settled on "It should be something that begins with idealistic goals, and then spins off into a quagmire. It will need to be a memorial that can remain endless, as a tribute to an endless war."

A memorial to an endless war is an interesting prospect. It's been said that war is a phenomenon like other inevitable, destructive forces of nature—fires, hurricanes—although war is, of course, a part of human nature. Perhaps for the right artist, this will be an opportunity to make the truest war memorial possible, a monument to this fault in our nature.

If I had my way, I would get rid of all America's war memorials and combine them into a single black wall of reflective granite, like Maya Lin's winning entry (number 1,026) for the Vietnam Veterans Memorial.

I'd place the wall around the Reflecting Pool, beneath the long shadow of the Washington Monument and Lincoln Memorial, the wall descending into the earth like something out of Dante. Etched into the wall would be names, and the very first would be Crispus Attucks, a black freeman shot dead by redcoats at the Boston Massacre. From there the wall would slope downward, each death taking it deeper into the earth, the angle of its descent defined by 1.3 million names, our nation's cumulative war dead. The wall itself would be endless. When a new war began, we wouldn't erect a new monument. We wouldn't have debates about real estate on the mall. Instead, we'd continue our descent. (If there's one thing you learn in the military, it's how to dig into the earth.) Deeper and deeper our wars would take us. To remember the fresh dead, we would have to walk past all the ones who came before. The human cost would be forever displayed in one

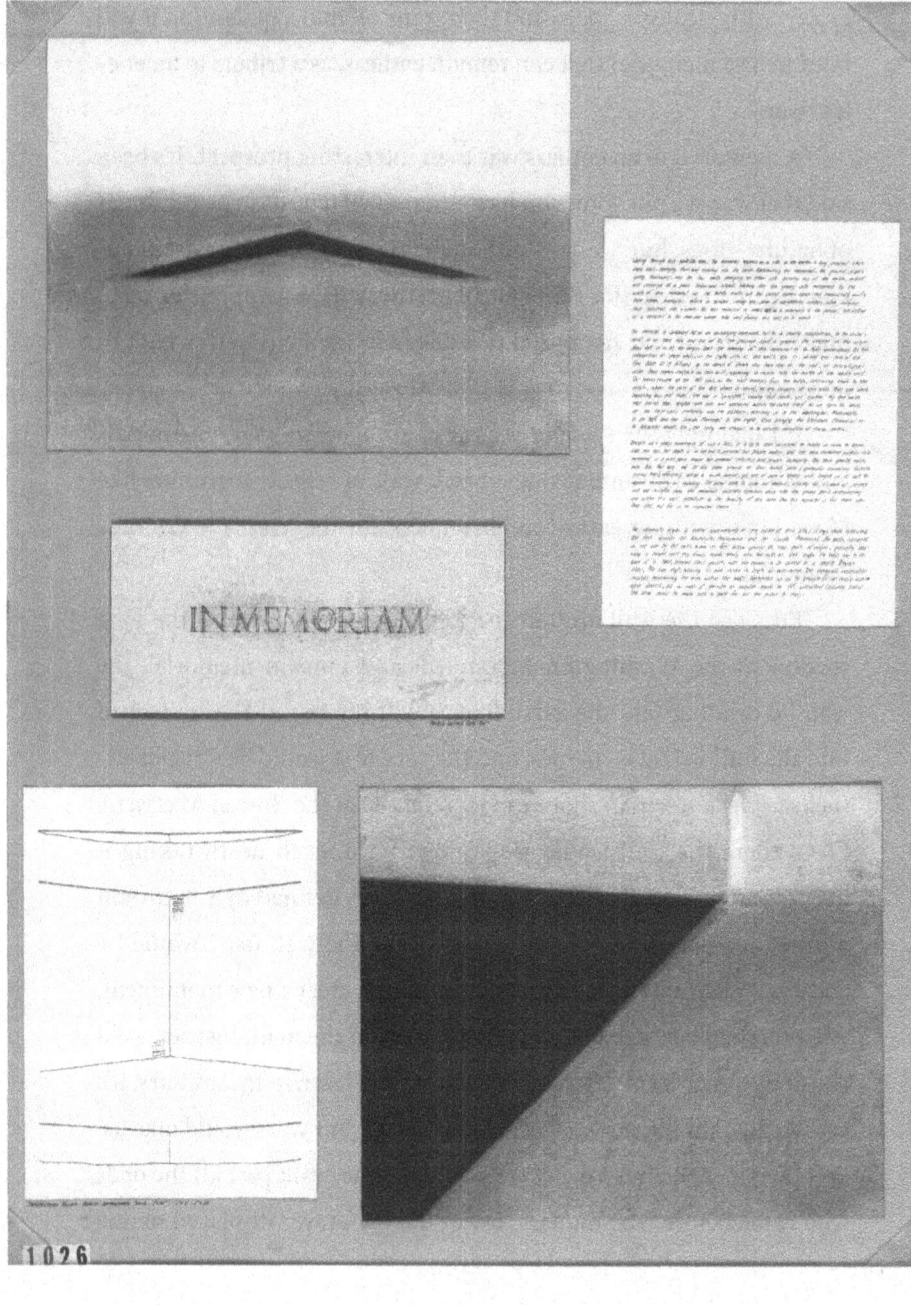

monumental place, as opposed to scattered disconnectedly across the mall.

The memorial would have a real-world function too. Imagine if Congress passed legislation ensuring that every time a president signed a troop deployment order, he or she would have to descend into this pit. There, beside the very last name—the person most recently killed in defense of this country or its interests—would be a special pen, nothing fancy, but this pen would be the only pen by law that could sign such an order.

It's been some time since I've thought about that run on the mall with Seth. My wife and I are sitting on the rooftop of the Danieli, talking about our children, when my phone rings. The caller ID reads *Unknown*. Typically, I wouldn't answer at dinner. But the past few days have been anything but typical. My wife waits patiently as I take the call. "Hello?"

"Hey, man, it's Seth. Listen, I'm in Kabul, at HKIA." Seth had—along with Congressman Peter Meijer—controversially hopped on a military flight. The two wanted to see the situation for themselves. "If you need anything," he adds, "I'm going to be here for the next few hours and might be able to help."

If only Seth had arrived last night. He might have been able to get one of the airport gates open for us. After that failure, we haven't scheduled an attempt to enter the airport tonight, and will not, until we find a more reliable way to get through the gates, one that doesn't rely on a convoy that presents such a large and dangerous target. Seth is earnest in his desire to help. I imagine I'm one of dozens of similar calls he's making. He says that if anything changes, I should hit him up on Signal. He'll do whatever he can. I'm glad he's made the trip and tell him so.

"Who was that?" asks my wife after I hang up.

"Seth. He's in Kabul."

The psychic disconnect of where we are versus where Seth has called from imposes a brief silence. Then my wife says, "Do you think he's okay?" She doesn't express the nature of her concern with any specificity, but she doesn't have to. She has seen over the past few days how the war has tugged me back into its orbit. She has seen the same among friends of ours who are veterans. And now, with Seth, she's seen a veteran not only psychically return to Afghanistan but physically return there as well. Granted, he sits on the House Armed Services Committee, so one might argue he isn't a veteran returning to war but rather a member of Congress executing the oversight duties of his office. But what really differentiates Seth isn't the office he holds, but that he had access to a flight, the same flight so many of us want to board so we might return to Afghanistan to finish our war, to count ourselves present in this, its final act.

The final act of this war has been more difficult than the final act of my other war, in Iraq. When in 2014 cities like Fallujah fell to the Islamic State, it didn't have nearly the same emotional impact as watching the Taliban blitzkrieg through Afghanistan. Not long after Kabul fell, I was on the phone with another friend, Josh, a Naval Academy graduate. He'd also fought in Fallujah and then went on to fight in western Afghanistan. The two of us were struggling to understand our disparate reactions to the ends of these two wars. We had served in the same Marine special operations unit and had advised the same group of Afghan commandos within one year of each other. Our experiences in the Corps tracked closely. We'd fought in the same battles, earned the same campaign ribbons, and had many of the same mentors and friends. We also had sons who were around the same age. The ostensible reason for our call that day was to coordinate the logistics of a long-planned trip to take our two sons to Annapolis to watch Navy play Air Force in football on the twentieth anniversary of 9/11, a game that would now take on a very different resonance given recent events in Afghanistan.

"Has this been harder for you than Iraq?" I'd asked Josh.

"Definitely harder."

"Why is that?"

Although Josh and I had a great deal in common, one area where our experience differed was that Josh had been medically retired from the Marines. He'd already earned two Purple Hearts when he was wounded a third time, after an A-10 Thunderbolt flying overhead had fired its 30 mm cannon off target. Fragmentation from the cannon's rounds nearly cost Josh his right leg below the knee. To walk he wears a brace. But the reason Josh gave had nothing to do with his final set of wounds. "Afghanistan was the good war," he said. "No one attacked us from Iraq."

In our country's history, we've only fought two wars predicated on an attack against our homeland. The first was the Second World War, a conflict that ended with the unconditional surrender of our enemies. The second was the war in Afghanistan, a conflict that is ending with *our* unconditional surrender. And our enemy, the one setting the terms of our departure, isn't Nazi Germany or Imperial Japan; it's 75,000 Taliban fighters. They are dictating the terms of withdrawal to the largest, most powerful military on earth. It's a bitter thing. A humiliating thing. An added irony is that one could make a credible case that our other war, in Iraq (though predicated on a faulty premise), was the war we didn't lose. I certainly wouldn't go so far as to say we won the Iraq War, but I also wouldn't go so far as to say that we lost it, particularly as the country has now successfully held four consecutive sets of parliamentary elections without any meaningful violence. Yes, the Iraqi government is plenty dysfunctional. But so is our own. America's mixed outcome in Iraq paired with our unequivocal loss in Afghanistan feels not only like a national indictment, but also a generational one.

When my wife's father sat on the rooftop of the Danieli after his war, these questions did not exist for him. In that way we are different. Fighting in a war is one experience, but winning or losing your war is another experience entirely. This is where he and I diverge.

My wife and I enjoy our meal. We make an effort to talk of other things. We stay later than I imagined we would, the two of us savoring the view, the city, the magic of this place. Eventually, our server brings us the bill. My wife stops him. Would he mind taking a photograph of

the two of us? We step to the railing. The city is below. The water is beyond us. The Salute stands to our side, its dome fitting like a third person in the frame. Our server takes the picture. He hands my wife her phone. She smiles sweetly when she sees the photo. She will send it to her mother. She says, "It will remind her of Daddy."

SCENE III

Firebase Thomas, Herat Province, 2008

After Momez's death, the major came to visit us. He had returned from Bagram to his headquarters in Herat the week prior. His convoy of four vehicles now arrived in a cloud of dust at our firebase, a three-hour drive south, at a little before lunch. When the major and his convoy dismounted in our gravel parking lot, I could see Tubes among them. He swung down from the door of an RG-33, a new super-armored, monster-truck-size fantasia of a fighting vehicle designed to survive the worst IEDs. Unlike our Humvees, the RG-33 had a remote turret that allowed the gunner to sit safely buttoned up within the steel confines of the vehicle. It also had a powerful suite of radios, which allowed Tubes better communications with distant aircraft. The RG-33 looked mean, vengeful, the type of vehicle Hollywood might design for a Marvel movie but which had instead found its way into our war.

The major was annoyed when he arrived. On the drive down, his communications with Tubes had proven spotty. What good was Tubes's new suite of ultrapowerful radios if the major's Humvee couldn't talk with them? When I approached the major, I could hear him telling Tubes that it was a problem they'd need to solve. I crossed the parking lot and welcomed the major. I told him that we had lunch ready. He thanked me and we walked to the mess tent. Tubes walked with us. His mustache seemed to have grown back a little. When I mentioned this to Tubes at lunch, he gave its end a playful twist. His hands seemed to be healing too.

We sat in the mess tent at a picnic table with a vinyl tablecloth. Afghan workers had prepared our meal in stainless-steel vats. We scooped food onto plastic plates and ate with plastic utensils. Willy and Super Dave also sat at the table with us. The major was asking Super Dave about his team and how they were holding up. Although we were all feeling the loss of Momez, he was Dave's soldier, a member of the special forces, not one of us, not a Marine. Dave was sanguine and appreciative of the major's interest. He didn't tell the major about how some in his team were asking why no one else in the vehicle had tried to save Momez, why it had fallen to Tubes. Dave felt his team sergeant could have gotten to Momez sooner. But he hadn't. (When Dave later fired him, he said that was why.)

Everyone was happy to see Tubes. Lang and Redbone came over and asked how he was doing, as did Angry Dave and a few others from the special forces. Everyone knew Tubes had done all that he could. His still-bandaged hands were a testament to that. Our table finished eating and got up at the same time. We were going to walk over to the TOC (said "tock"), the tactical operations center, where I'd take the major through our upcoming missions, to include a series of helicopter raids we were planning just to the south of us, in the Zerkoh Valley, a cluster of hamlets that had become a haven for Taliban fighters after a controversial battle there had led to the Karzai government calling it off-limits to both Afghan and US military forces a year ago.

On our way to the TOC, the major asked me to hang back with him for a minute. "I've got one thing I want to talk over with you." He stepped off the gravel footpath between the TOC and the mess tent, toward some dusty trees where we'd be out of view. As I followed the major, I caught Tubes giving me a sympathetic look, as if he knew what was coming, as if the major had previewed for him the talk we were about to have.

"What's up, sir?" I was trying to sound upbeat.

He crossed his arms over his chest. "You want to tell me what happened in Shewan?"

I slipped my hands in my pockets. "What do you mean, sir?"

"We don't leave our people behind."

"We didn't leave anyone behind."

"I ordered you to go back and get Sergeant Nunez."

I now planted my hands on my hips and half-pivoted away from the major. "Sir, all of our vehicles except for two were towing a downed vehicle. I only had those two vehicles to go back into Shewan with. If we'd tried that, we would've taken more casualties, possibly more dead, and made the situation worse. And in the end the other team was able to—"

The major cut me off. "He was *your* responsibility."

"And so was everyone else. I wasn't trying to disobey an order. I was trying to let you understand how precarious our situation was."

"I understood the situation." The major's arms remained crossed over his chest. When he spoke, he hardly opened his mouth. "I was there."

"Sir," I said, "you were in fucking Bagram."

I stood there and took the rest of my dressing-down. The major told me that it didn't matter that he'd been in Bagram. He could've been on the moon for all he cared. He was my commanding officer and he'd given me an order. I hadn't followed that order, or at least hadn't followed it in the way he'd wanted me to. He pointed out that his instincts—even if he was in Bagram—had proven correct because our sister team was ultimately able to recover Momez's body without incident. Our sister team had—according to the major—completed a mission that should've been completed by us.

He finished by saying, "No one's doubting your courage here. But I do doubt your judgment. Don't let it happen again." I asked him if that was all. He said that it was. And we walked toward the TOC, where I briefed him on our upcoming mission in the Zerkoh Valley. After the briefings, there was some discussion as to whether the major and his headquarters would stay for dinner. Willy thought we might have some steaks in the large, refrigerated shipping container where we stored our food. Our cooks checked, but the steaks wouldn't arrive until our next resupply flight. The major decided they would return to Herat instead. Tubes stood outside in our gravel parking lot waiting for Redbone to make some final adjustments to his radios in the RG-33, so they wouldn't have the same communications problems they'd had before. Tubes pulled me to the side. "You okay?" he asked.

"Yeah, fine. Sorry about the steaks, though."

He laughed; we'd do the steaks another time. Then he asked what the major had said. So I told him, specifically the bit about not doubting my courage but only my judgment. "The funny thing," I said, "is that I've come to feel it's the reverse. The longer this war goes on, the more I trust my judgment but the more I doubt my courage."

Before Tubes could answer, Redbone popped his head out of the cab of the RG-33. He gripped the radio handset and called down to us. "Hey, I fixed it. You should be coming in loud and clear now."

SCENE IV

Torcello, Venice

The six of us follow our tour guide down a gravel path. She is walking backward, explaining the history of this place. Torcello is the oldest inhabited island in the municipality of Venice. After Attila the Hun sacked the port city of Altinum, in 452, the Roman inhabitants fled into the lagoon. They spread out, urban refugees, finding sanctuary on the water from invasions and wars. They brought their church with them, and in 638, the bishop of Altino seated himself in Torcello, building what we are about to see, the basilica of Santa Maria Assunta. For almost five hundred years, Torcello thrived as a seat of power and commerce. At its height, it's estimated to have had 35,000 inhabitants, and was far more powerful than Venice. But one age slips to the next. Environmental changes (a rise in the water level) and a pandemic (the fourteenth-century black death) devastate Torcello. Its inhabitants

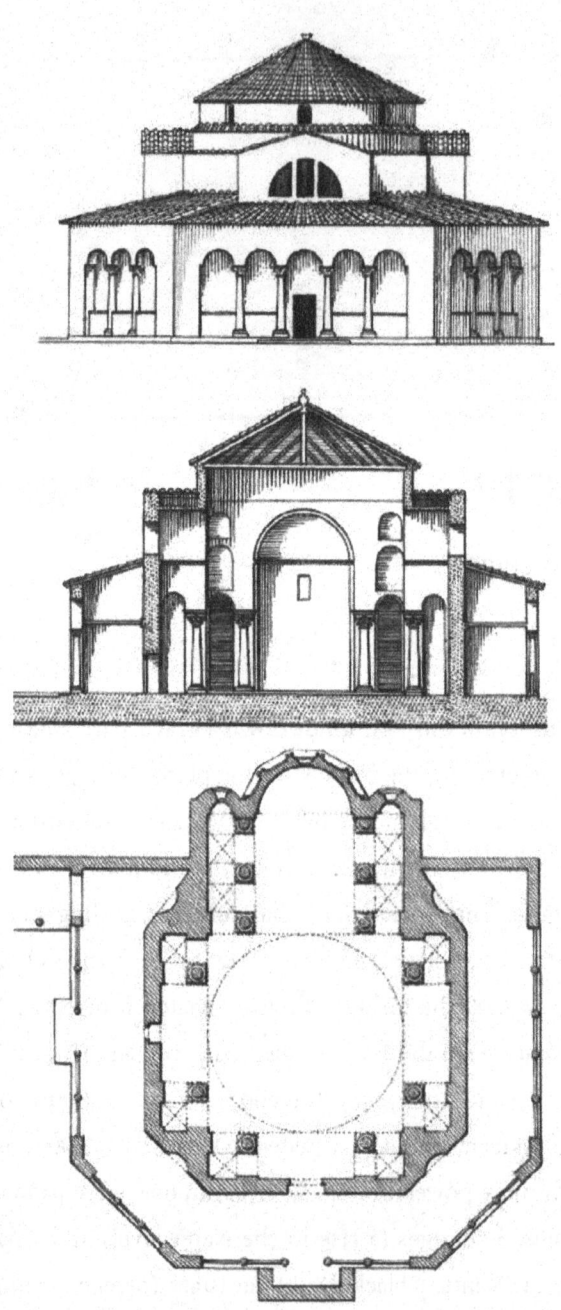

again flee. Today, Torcello boasts a population of twelve. The spire of its basilica comes into view above the treetops.

I walk a few steps behind my family, talking on my phone. A friend of mine, Richard, called me this morning to see if I could lend him a hand. His nephew's college roommate served in the army, with the special forces. The roommate—whom I've never met—has an interpreter who is trapped in Kabul. His name is Shah, and it's not just him that Richard is trying to get out, but also Shah's wife, Forozan, who is seven months pregnant. After our failed attempt at the South Gate, I've told Richard that I'm not sure what help I can offer, but Richard and Shah are working every angle possible, to include one that he's asking my opinion about as we chat on the phone. Shah and his wife are in a safe house maintained by the Canadians, who are attempting to evacuate them from Kabul but with little success. Shah has been told through a contact he has with the former Afghan royal family that if he goes to HKIA and tells the Marines there a certain password, they'll let him in. Shah wants to travel to the airport and try his luck with the whole royal password thing. Richard, a successful and imminently pragmatic businessman, finishes explaining the situation and asks, "What do you think? Does this sound viable to you?"

"No," I say. "It doesn't sound viable." What I don't say, but what I think, is that this sounds desperate, and that it's only further evidence of the utter collapse that has occurred across Afghanistan. If the Canadians think they can evacuate Shah and his wife, he should stay in the safe house. When the call for him to leave comes from the Canadians, it's only going to come once. If he's at the airport trying to convince a group of strung-out, trigger-happy Marines about the authenticity of a secret password given to him by the Afghan royal family, he could, potentially, miss his only chance to get out. Or worse.

Richard agrees but says he's having a hard time convincing Shah to stay put. Shah doesn't have much faith in the Canadians at this point, or the Americans. He'd rather put his faith in the Afghan royal family—deposed fifty years ago—along with some dubious secret passwords. Of course, Shah's mistrust shouldn't come as a surprise. The end of our war in Afghanistan represents the end of twenty years of promises: to local leaders who allied themselves with us at great personal risk, to women who'd taken steps toward equality, to Afghan soldiers like Shah who'd fought to keep their country from falling apart, and to the government of Afghanistan itself. Yet this isn't one-sided. Years of Afghan corruption and double-dealing with US adversaries such as Iran and Pakistan strained our relations with the Afghan government under both presidents Hamid Karzai and Ashraf Ghani. In war, the Afghans were not always reliable partners. They siphoned off billions of dollars in aid. They participated in the opium trade. Incompetence in their high command bordered on negligence. The betrayals—and there have been plenty—certainly run both ways.

The peace deal negotiated by the Trump administration with the Taliban was one of these betrayals. From the outset, the Afghan government wasn't a party to these negotiations, which were held directly between the United States and the Taliban. This strategy resembled the flawed American negotiations during the Vietnam War, which led to the 1973 Paris Peace Accords, in which National Security Adviser Henry Kissinger cut out the government of South Vietnam. To end that war, we negotiated directly with North Vietnam and presented final terms to South Vietnam's president Nguyễn Văn Thiệu as a fait accompli. He had days to accept them or America threatened to cut off aid to the South, whose government Washington had long treated with little regard. Those terms were, ultimately, accepted, which further undermined the legitimacy of Thiệu's already fragile government and paved the way for the fall of Saigon only two years later.

In Doha, American negotiators treated Kabul the same way. The Trump administration's agreement with the Taliban, signed February 29, 2020, fatally delegitimized President Ghani and his central government. The agreement released five thousand Taliban prisoners without the Afghan government's consent. In paragraph after paragraph, the United States refused to recognize the Taliban, beginning each clause of the agreement with "The Islamic Emirate of Afghanistan, which is not recognized by the United States as a state and is known as the Taliban, will . . ." However, US negotiators went on to contradict themselves, gesturing toward their expectation that the Taliban would take over Afghanistan when they introduced the following measure into the Doha agreement: "The Islamic Emirate of Afghanistan, which is not recognized by the United States as a state and is known as the Taliban, will not provide visas, passports, travel permits, or other legal documents to those who pose a threat to the security of the United States and its allies to enter Afghanistan."

Only a sovereign nation has the authority to issue legal travel documents. In the same sentence, the United States both denies and acknowledges the prospect of Taliban sovereignty over Afghanistan. Imagine reading that language as a member of the Afghan government. Is it any wonder, then, that our Afghan allies believe we are speaking out of both sides of our mouth? Is it any wonder that people like Shah are done with our promises? Should I really be surprised that he won't stay put at a Canadian safe house, that he's concluded our promises are thin and has decided to try his own luck at the airport?

Before I get off the phone with Richard, he asks if I've heard anything else about convoys headed into HKIA. Unfortunately, I haven't. Since our failed bid at the South Gate, the consensus increasingly seems to be that large convoys are no longer practical given the crush of people at the airport. Earlier in the day, I'd sent Lieutenant Colonel Chris Richardella a message over Signal, asking about conditions at the North Gate, if maybe he and his Marines could facilitate us getting a few people inside. I still haven't heard back from him, but I tell Richard that I'll let him know if I do. We hang up.

I rejoin my family, who've already entered the basilica. They stand among the registers of angels, demons, and saints that populate the heavily mosaicked walls. The most dominant color is gold. Age dulls its shine. Our guide is standing in the basilica's narthex; this, she explains, was a type of separate lobby area typical of churches dating to the premedieval, or Byzantine, period. From the narthex, we face toward the basilica's main apse. Here, adorned in more gold relief, is a famous eleventh-century mosaic of the Virgin Mary cradling the infant Jesus in her arms. The Virgin points to her child as the way to salvation. Our guide explains that this church was designed so that when you entered, a dramatic image of salvation would confront you, overwhelm you, and entice you deeper inside. Opposite the apse is the west wall, which contains the second most dramatic mosaic, a depiction of the Crucifixion of Christ, a Harrowing of Hell, and then, in the lower panels, the Last Judgment. The west wall, she explains, was designed to create an entirely different effect. "When you entered the basilica," she says, "this would be behind you, so you would not see it at first. All you would see is the Virgin, your salvation. But on your way out, when you exit, this is the moment when you would be reminded of all of your sins."

In the bottom right corner of the west wall, very close to the exit, is a seven-paneled mosaic. Our guide explains that this was—by eleventh-century standards—a graphic depiction of the seven deadly sins. My children are captivated by the gory images. A pile of decapitated heads adorned with jeweled earrings and necklaces represents

greed. Skulls with venomous snakes slithering through the eye sockets represent envy. Our guide explains each panel with a ghoulish delight. The children are eager to know which of the sins is the worst.

"They're all pretty bad," I say.

The guide is quick to correct me. "Actually, among the ancient Christians, it was believed that one sin was the greatest among them all." She points to the top panel, which is the largest of the seven. In it, Lucifer sits on his throne, which is ornamented with the heads of rams and other pagan symbols. He is surrounded by the flames of hell. On his lap is a child, the Antichrist, cradled in the same adoring way that the Virgin cradles the infant Jesus on the opposite wall. Two avenging angels prod Lucifer's victims with spears into the flames of hell. Here, they are not only tormented by the flames but also by swarms of winged demons who hover above Lucifer, clutching the decapitated heads they are ready to deliver to him. These victims all have one thing in common. Each wears a crown. They are monarchs, the leaders of nations. Our guide explains their sin. "Pride," she says. "The ancient Christians believed that all sins derived from this one. So they placed this image here. A little reminder as you walked out the door."

We have left the basilica and are wandering its grounds when my phone rings. It is Lieutenant Colonel Richardella. "Sorry it's taken me a while to get back to you," he says. "Things have been busy." He explains that his infantry battalion still holds the North Gate. He can't get any vehicles through, but there is a small access point—nothing more than a door—and if I can get people to that access point on foot, his Marines can step out into the crowd, snatch them, and bring them inside the airport.

"Let me get organized," I say. "After that I'll hit you up on Signal and you can let me know the best time to send folks to the gate."

He says that sounds good, and then I ask him if his Marine battalion is the only one at the airport. Richardella explains that there's another battalion; that the two units are part of a larger Marine task force, commanded by a full colonel. When he mentions the colonel's name, I recognize it immediately. Richardella says, "Didn't you work for him once, in Afghanistan, when he was a major?"

SCENE V

Firebase Thomas, Herat Province, 2008

Our operation in the Zerkoh Valley had proven a success. We'd launched a series of helicopter and overland raids, and the Taliban, who for months relied on the valley as a sanctuary, had fled. The Afghan military and police were already reasserting their control, negotiating the locations for a chain of new outposts. The Afghan commandos— and we, their advisers—were riding high. It'd taken us weeks to secure the valley, and after we did, congratulations had poured in from the highest levels, to include the general in command of all allied troops in Afghanistan. Before the operation began, Super Dave and I had needed to brief the general in person. He'd made a point of telling us that he'd had a hard time convincing President Karzai to green-light the operation. Karzai was leery of the possibility of civilian casualties and re-enmeshing himself in the complex tribal politics that had allowed the Zerkoh Valley to become a Taliban sanctuary in the first place. The general had needed our operation to be flawless. His parting words for us were "Don't fuck it up." And we hadn't. Now it seemed we could do no wrong.

The major was pleased with us too. We worked for him, and so our success was his success. Victories like Zerkoh Valley replaced defeats like Shewan. We moved on. Because what other choice was there?

With the night raids, air strikes, and firefights of the Zerkoh operation behind us, we had transitioned into the more civic-minded portion of the mission. In this, the Afghan commandos would now take a back seat. The major and his headquarters, however, would play a more central role, negotiating long-term security arrangements in the valley with the very same local power brokers who had only weeks before collaborated with the Taliban. In US military speak, this type of mission had a name, *key leader engagement*—and if it had a name, it had an acronym: KLE.

Only a few days after the last of the commandos withdrew from the Zerkoh Valley, the major and his headquarters had one such KLE scheduled. They departed from Herat early that morning, which placed their convoy of a half dozen vehicles at our firebase in time for a late lunch. They ate in a rush. The major, who understood how tentative our gains were in the valley, didn't want to arrive late to the KLE. He was anxious about further alienating the village elders, whose patience was running thin after they'd endured several weeks of fighting in their valley. Those in the major's headquarters, however, would only be rushed so much. They craved a decent meal. I can't remember what was served in our mess tent that day, but I recall the headquarters Marines trickling back to their vehicles, disappointed. This included Tubes, who was sitting on the hood of the major's Humvee. He'd taken up smoking and offered me a Marlboro.

"You riding with the major now?" I asked.

"Don't get me started," he said wryly, but then proceeded to explain how they'd never quite been able to get the radio suite in the RG-33 to communicate seamlessly with the major's Humvee. They'd tried everything, wiring and rewiring the radios in every way imaginable. Nothing had worked. In the end, the major lost his patience. Tubes would ride in the major's vehicle, crammed into the seat next to him, even if that meant Tubes couldn't communicate as well with the aircraft overhead.

I said, "That sucks."

Tubes shrugged and then changed the subject. "Whatever happened to those steaks you guys promised us?" He complained a bit more about the quality of his lunch and then proceeded to deliver a minor guilt trip, one in which I had proven myself an inadequate host by offering him and the headquarters Marines an inedible meal. "We're going to roll back through here after the KLE. That should be about dinnertime. You could redeem yourself with some steaks."

"You're overestimating my influence with the dinner menu," I said. "It's Willy, not me, who is the keeper of the steaks." But I promised Tubes that I'd ask about it. We were due for a steak night anyway, and last I'd checked, we had some saved in our refrigeration container.

The headquarters convoy soon departed in a cloud of late-afternoon dust. They unspooled out our front gate and drove the remaining hour into the valley. With them gone, the firebase felt quiet again. My room was right off the TOC. While I sat at my desk, I could hear the staccato radio transmissions as they called out checkpoints. Willy came by and I asked about the steaks. He told me our cooks were already preparing them. Several dozen emails and a couple of phone calls later, it was dinnertime. But headquarters was still in the valley. We'd have to eat without them. I had the radio-watch relay that we'd have dinner ready for them when they came back. I walked with Willy and Super Dave down to the mess tent. The meal was a feast. We sat for a long time afterward, talking and laughing with full bellies. It was the height of summer and still light as we strolled back outside. That's when I spotted Redbone up the gravel path, in the direction of the TOC. Our eyes connected and he ran straight toward me.

"Sir," he said under his breath, "headquarters requested a medevac. It sounds like they just hit an IED." When I asked Redbone how bad it was, he handed me a Post-it note. Scrawled on it was the entire request. But all I saw was a single kill number—*Lima Alpha*: Lawton . . . Tubes—as well as his medevac status: routine.

SCENE VI

A hotel room in Venice

Shah and his wife never return to the Canadian safe house. Their plan—of using the passwords from their contact with the Afghan royal family—has failed. Afterward, they spend the night at a gas station near the airport. While Shah and his wife rest at the gas station, my wife and I pack up our children for the last leg of our journey. We have a domestic flight scheduled the next morning, which will take us south, where we plan to spend a few pleasant days near the seaside. As we pack, I'm swapping messages on Signal with Richard (who is in touch with Shah), with Richardella (who has confirmed his Marines will be ready to help us in the morning), and with Ian (who has a small group of his own evacuees led by an Afghan woman, Adeeba, that he needs to link up with Shah).

The plan is for everyone to enter the North Gate together. But Ian's group is exhausted and reluctant to leave the safety of a mosque where they've hunkered down for the night. Shah, for his part, is reluctant to search out Ian's group. His pregnant wife is struggling to stay on her feet. She's exhausted from their earlier attempt to enter the North Gate and needs rest. Shah refuses to wander too far from her. For hours on Signal, Ian and Richard swap messages, trying to sort out this linkup. The two of them have never met.

Earlier in the day, Ian and I had spoken on the phone. Both of us had remarked on how surreal this increasingly crowdsourced evacuation had become, how it had placed us in chat groups with people we'd never met and how we'd found ourselves scrambling to evacuate Afghans whom we knew only tenuously—often through the referral of Americans whom we knew only slightly less tenuously. It infuriated Ian how our government had no system in place, how the leveraging of personal networks was what determined whether someone could get into the airport or not, how Afghans would live or die based on the contact list in their cell phone. Ian said it reminded him of the war, which was waged in a similarly personal and networked fashion. He reminded me of the targets we used to chase, in some cases for years, those al-Qaeda cell leaders and Taliban commanders. We became familiar with them, the relationships having a similar quality of acquaintance, and we would hear in our reporting that our adversaries hazily knew who we were too, how they understood what units and—in certain cases—what people were rotating in and out of familiar Afghan bases. The war—so long forgotten—had been fought on intimate terms.

And now it was ending that way too.

It is late. Of Adeeba and her group, Ian writes, *They are smoked and trying to rest before pushing. Everyone too tired to move and too scared not to.*

Exhausted myself, I fall asleep.

The next morning, my wife and I are hustling our children through breakfast, out of our hotel, and into a taxi when another message arrives. It's the one we've been waiting for, from Richardella:

Team, how many do we have ready to come through the North Gate?

SCENE VII

Zerkoh Valley, Herat Province, 2008

Standard operating procedure was to keep black vinyl bags in the back of each truck, out of sight. His remains had been zipped up in one of those bags. It had been placed nearby, on a patch of charred sand, not far from the crater. The destroyed Humvee sat on the lip of the crater. Blood, like spilled paint, stained the side of the hood and wheel well. The remaining vehicles in the convoy had fanned out, their machine guns refuting the IED and the valley's insult like a piece of staircase wit. The major sat inside the RG-33, dazed like a prizefighter between rounds, clutching a radio handset he wasn't talking into. We had gotten down there in less than an hour. You could still smell the explosives in the air, the acrid mix of cordite and gasoline. Everyone was speaking in whispers. Tubes was dead.

We needed to remove all the sensitive items from the wrecked Humvee, which mostly included Tubes's encrypted radios. We then needed to rig up the Humvee so we could tow it back to our firebase. We worked into the night, a circle of our headlights illuminating the wreckage. I learned from others what had happened: how headquarters was running late for the KLE; how, to arrive on time, they'd chosen to take a dirt road that led them into a wadi; how they'd accounted for this risk by placing the IED-resistant RG-33 at the front of the convoy because it could safely absorb most blasts; how they hadn't accounted for the RG-33's narrower wheelbase; how the Humvee's wider wheelbase had run over the pressure plate and triggered the IED as they came out of the wadi; how the explosives must've been placed directly under Tubes's seat; how the major had been sitting next to Tubes and had survived; how if Tubes's radios had been working, he would've been in the RG-33 instead of with the major.

Periodically, as we worked, I jogged over to the major, to update him on our progress. He remained seated in the RG-33, still clutching his handset but not making any transmissions. What transmission could unwind the *should'ves* and *could'ves* of that night? Tubes should not have died. They could have taken a different route. Or Tubes could've ridden in the RG-33. I wanted to snatch the handset away from the major. What was the point of holding on to it? There was nothing left to say about what'd happened in this valley, just as there was nothing left to say about Shewan, or that any of us could say about any of this. If he and I had been friends, if he hadn't been my boss—if he had been, say, Tubes—I would've told him, *Is what it is*. But he wasn't. Instead, I quietly asked Redbone to get on the radio. He would pass our situation report up to our higher headquarters in Bagram.

We convoyed through the valley in silence. Tubes's body was in the back of another Humvee. The next morning, a C-130 would land at the dusty airstrip near our firebase for the first leg of his journey home. Until then, we would need to keep him somewhere. Our hospital corpsman suggested we use our refrigeration container as a makeshift morgue.

Immediately on returning to our firebase, we placed Tubes's remains inside the refrigeration container on a stretcher. We cleared out a corner for him, in the back. This was the best we could do, at least for now. Each of us paid our respects, and I soon found myself alone with him in the cold. I crouched down and touched the vinyl bag. I was saying goodbye when the door swung open. The sun was, by now, coming up. I squinted into the light, toward a silhouetted figure who apologized as he quickly stepped inside. It was one of our Afghan cooks. He was so sorry to interrupt, but he needed to grab a few things. He'd been told by Willy to go back and see if it was possible to reheat the meal from the night before.

SCENE VIII

A taxi to the airport

My wife counts our bags. Then she counts our children. We have everyone and everything. Shoulder to shoulder, we load into the taxi. She also counts the time, which she's made sure we'll have plenty of, so we won't miss our flight. I've often teased her about how early she makes us arrive at any airport. But because of her we've never missed a flight, and likely never will.

Shah is also on his way to the airport, as are the eight Afghans from Ian's group. Richardella, who is inside HKIA, posts in our chat, *Let's shoot for 1300. Consolidate who you can and tell them to move toward the front of that side gate.*

Our chat has a new addition, Danny. He is the army veteran turned college roommate of my friend Richard's nephew. He is the one who fought alongside Shah in Afghanistan. We've added him because he is in direct contact with Shah. After Richardella sends his message, I post, *Rgr. Ian, copy? Danny, copy?*

Both reply, *copy.*

The Marines will need to be able to recognize Shah in the crowd. To signal them, Shah writes his name in blue block letters on a piece of white printer paper along with that of his wife, Forozan. It's the best he can do. Danny posts a photograph of Shah's paper sign to the chat, so Richardella can pass it along to the Marines who will be looking for him.

Ian is struggling to get in touch with his eight at the mosque. He posts, *I've lost comms with Adeeba and group. Her WhatsApp was last seen an hour ago, don't want to hold you guys up.*

Richardella posts, *Let's get as many in at once as possible. This site is burned. I want to get this group in before we shut it down for a while.*

Ian asks Danny if he knows what Adeeba said to Shah when they last spoke the night before.

When I arrive at the airport with my family, Danny still hasn't responded to Ian's question. The taxi driver is helping us unload our bags, and I am doing my best to pay attention to the chat and to help my wife count the bags and the children as we move into the terminal. We are at the ticket counter when a response from Danny finally arrives: *I think she just made contact . . . Stand by . . . She's close to the north gate . . . She called Shah . . . He is looking for her.*

Ian answers, *I needed that. Thanks.*

Danny posts a photograph taken by Shah to the group chat. It is of his perspective with relation to the North Gate. A pair of wheelbarrows sits in the foreground, filled with bottled water that vendors are selling to the desperate, exhausted crowds. Beyond the vendors, those trying to leave have pressed themselves against a concrete wall. The top of the wall is threaded with coils of concertina wire. At a distance, a single helmeted head wearing wraparound sunglasses pokes above the wall. The muzzle of a rifle is trained on the crowd. It's one of the Marines from 1/8, Richardella's battalion. Shah draws a big red arrow on the photograph pointed down at this Marine. When he shares it, Danny writes, *Working to get a better picture but this is what I got. Shah didn't want to get too close.*

Ian sends the photo to Adeeba. Their two groups are struggling to find each other at the North Gate. He writes, *Trying to talk her through sharing location with me on WhatsApp.*

My wife needs my passport. She has checked our bags at the ticket counter, and they are now printing out our boarding passes. "Didn't I already give my passport to you?" I ask, shifting my attention away from the phone. She shakes her head, no. In her hand are everyone else's passports except mine, and she reminds me how when she had offered to hold on to all of the passports at the beginning of the trip, I had insisted on keeping track of my own. I riffle through my pockets until I recall that I'd put the passport in my carry-on. I hand it to her and return to my phone, where I see that Richardella has posted another message: *The team needs to move to the fence gate. Get to the front and sit tight. How many are we extracting?*

I write, *Danny, I'm tracking you're: 2 pax. Ian, I am tracking you're: 8 pax. That's 10 pax total. Confirm.*

Both confirm the numbers traveling in their groups and that they are now headed to the side gate. Richardella posts, *Let us know when the group has linked up and are in position. We'll be ready.*

The crowd around the North Gate is a thick swaying mass, jammed chest to chest and shoulder to shoulder. In recent days, the Biden administration has publicly remarked that those with visas to the United States, as well as green card holders and American citizens, are free to enter the airport for processing. Except entering the airport is no small feat. The crowds are so dense, the environment so chaotic, that what we're asking Shah and Adeeba to do is the equivalent of finding each other in the crowd at a packed rock concert—say, the Rolling Stones at Altamont—and then working their way to the front of that crowd and then getting the attention of the band so they can be lifted up on stage.

Ten minutes have passed when Ian writes, *Update: Adeeba says she can see the gate and is trying to get there. I've tried to talk her through sharing location in WhatsApp, but for now seems better that she just keep moving. I will ping her in a few and reassess.*

Danny responds, *Shah is at location where tear gas was just dropped as a reference point for location.*

Another ten minutes go by. I am waiting in the security line with my family at the airport when Ian posts, *She seems far still.*

Danny writes, *Shah close to gate, but not pushed up so as to link up with Adeeba.*

Ian confirms that Adeeba is still struggling to get up to the gate. Danny tells him that Shah will keep waiting. Shah has never met Adeeba. She is a stranger to him, but he'll wait. Then Ian posts, *Appears to me she will get there right at 1300.*

Richardella pops up in the text: How many are ready to go?

Danny: Linkup with two groups happening at north gate now, stand by for confirmation.

Richardella: Roger, let us know. They can link arms, move to the front, and we'll bring them in.

A few more minutes pass. Danny comes up in the chat. It seems the linkup between Shah and Adeeba has occurred, though it's not entirely clear, and I post, *Roger, so I copy all 10 pax linked up and moving to North Gate now.*

Danny confirms this as I'm emptying my pockets into a dish, to include my cell phone. I pass through the metal detectors at security. In the few minutes it takes me to gather my things and walk with my family to the gate for our flight, the text chain proceeds like this:

Richardella: We're here and ready. What's signal of lead trace?

(I repost the sheet of paper with Shah and Forozan's names printed in blue block letters.)

Danny: Linking arms. Pushing to front now.

Richardella: Copy on all. We're ready.

(For good measure, I repost a photograph of Shah while Danny reposts a photograph of Forozan, so both will be more easily recognizable to the Marines.)

Richardella: This is what it looks like from our end. Canal to the south, t-walls north which is the vehicle entrance. Vendors are right behind the group in front of us.

(The photograph he posts is taken from down a narrow, open-air corridor, a ravine of barricades, dominated by a cement wall on one side and a chain-link fence on the other, which drops a dozen feet into a putrescent canal. Empty bottles of water, seemingly hurled over the wall by the crowd, as well as shreds of cardboard and rocks, litter the ground. Tangles of wire lurch toward one another as though frozen in

the act of collapse. Their contorted attitudes reinforce every conceivable point of vulnerability, from the tops of the walls to the opening of the single steel door at its far end. The plan is for the Marines to charge down this corridor, out into the crowd, and then to haul our group inside.)

Danny: Relayed your picture. Their view.

(The photograph is taken by Shah. He is wedged into the crowd, so the frame is mostly consumed by the backs of other people's heads. In the distance you can see a pair of Marines barricaded behind a concrete wall with a roll of concertina wire unspooled across its top and a security camera with its black orbed lens dangling overhead on a small crane.)

Richardella: They are in front of the vehicle entrance, the fence gate is to their left on the south side of the t-wall. They need to move back, go around, and swing left.

Danny: Rgr. Communicating it to him.

Richardella: The canal is to their left. That's the catching feature. Hit the canal and turn right. Come to the fenced gate.
(A minute of silence passes.)

Richardella: Got visual. Keep coming forward.

Danny: Lost comms he's moving.

Richardella: We're moving now. We see him.

Danny: On phone w Shah that's him.

Richardella: We have him.

Danny: I love you. Thank you sir.

I have since arrived at my gate. My son is sitting beside me, playing a World War II fighter pilot game on his iPad. He blasts Nazi Messerschmitts and Japanese Zeros out of the sky. The other children are doing much the same, playing games on their phones or their iPads, watching videos, gently bickering with one another, and generally killing the thirty or so minutes until we board our flight. My wife slips into the seat next to mine. "You okay?" she asks. I show her my phone. She scrolls through the past fifteen minutes or so of messages. It was said of my wife's father that he could cry at an ice hockey game, and the apple didn't fall far from the tree. I've seen my wife cry watching football. It's one of the many things I love about her. When she hands me back my phone, she is wiping tears from her eyes, and she says only, "Thank God."

At this, my son glances up at the two of us and asks, "Are you guys okay?"

"We're fine," says my wife. "Some people who your dad has been trying to help look like they're going to get out of Afghanistan."

"But that's good news," he says. "Why are you both crying?"

My wife places her hand on the back of my neck. Very quietly, she says, "I think I'm just happy for those people." Then she looks at me and adds, "And I'm happy for your dad."

My son sits up straight, flaring back his shoulders ever so slightly. He puts his hand on my shoulder. He considers me for a moment like a general reviewing one of his troopers in the ranks, and with all the seriousness, composure, and gravitas a nine-year-old boy might muster, he says, "Good work, Dad. I'm happy for you too." Then he goes back to his game.

In the chat, we're trying to confirm that everyone got through the gate, that in the chaos no one was inadvertently left behind. Ian reposts the manifest for Richardella to confirm. In addition to confirming the manifest and that consular services have now processed everyone into the airport, Richardella posts a selfie. Shah stands center frame with his left arm embracing Forozan. To their right is Richardella, whose arm is outstretched as he snaps the picture. He still wears his helmet and body armor, with a small and familiar 1st Battalion, 8th Marines unit crest Velcroed to his chest alongside his rank insignia. The eight others in the group are huddled around these three, cramming themselves into the frame. Their smiles are unrestrained.

Ian writes, *Heroes.*

I write the same.

Danny writes, *I'm crying. Heroes. There's the fucking mannnnn.*

Our flight is going to board soon. My wife asks me if I wouldn't mind grabbing us a few sandwiches, as we're going to miss lunch and who knows what they'll serve on the plane. I wander off into the terminal, to a small kiosk, where I wait in line. On a separate thread, just to Richardella, I write, *Rich, on a side note, I was wondering which of your companies got them: A, B, C, Wpns? Just as an alum. Really damn fine work. I'm so grateful to you and those 1/8 Marines.*

He doesn't answer right away. He's busy, of course. I pick out a few sandwiches, some waters, a treat for each of the kids. In my pocket, I feel my phone ping with Richardella's response but need to finish paying. I take my change from the cashier and, with my arms full, manage to find a place to sit down. I fish out my phone. Rich has written, *Your old company of course. Anything for a Beirut Marine.*

My two wars, which spanned two decades, seem to collide with each other in this message. The force pins me to this seat in the airport. I sit there with the bag of sandwiches at my feet, in a daze, while whole packs of travelers seem to float by. I am staring vacantly across the terminal when my son eventually finds me. "Dad," he says, "it's time to go. We're boarding."

He and I rush to the gate. When I arrive at my seat on the plane, there's a last message posted by Danny: *Any idea where they are flying to?*

ACT IV

THE ABBEY GATE

I know my decision will be criticized, but I would rather take all that criticism than pass this decision on to another president of the United States—yet another one—a fifth one.

—PRESIDENT JOE BIDEN
EAST ROOM OF THE WHITE HOUSE
AUGUST 16, 2021

SCENE I

Washington, D.C., 2020

In *New York Times v. United States*, the landmark 1971 case that permitted the publication of the Pentagon Papers, Supreme Court Justice Hugo Black in his majority opinion wrote, "Only a free and unrestrained press can effectively expose deception in government. And paramount among the responsibilities of a free press is the duty to prevent any part of the government from deceiving the people and sending them off to distant lands to die." In an echo of that time, and after a contested legal proceeding, the *Washington Post* releases "The Afghanistan Papers: A Secret History of the War." It's a trove of hundreds of unpublished interviews on the prosecution of the conflict with senior-level officials conducted by the Special Inspector General for Afghanistan Reconstruction, known as SIGAR.

The release coincides with the Trump administration's renewed negotiations with the Taliban, in 2019. Analysts speculate whether the Afghanistan Papers could have a similar galvanizing effect as the Pentagon Papers, which sped the conclusion of the Vietnam War. This seems to be the imperative behind their release. Craig Whitlock, the investigative journalist responsible for the reporting, writes in a preamble, "The specter of Vietnam has hovered over Afghanistan from the start."

Parallels certainly exist between the two wars. The US-backed governments in both countries suffered from endemic corruption. Our adversaries enjoyed sanctuaries next door (Cambodia and Laos for Vietnam, Pakistan for Afghanistan). The drug trade exploded in each country as a result of the war. Most profoundly, in Afghanistan as in Vietnam, we disastrously misunderstood the central objective of our adversaries. For the Vietcong and North Vietnamese, the war was one of national liberation, while we Americans associated it with domino theory and transnational communism. For the Taliban, the war has also been one of national liberation, in which the expulsion of foreigners from Afghanistan proves an enduring organizing principle, while we Americans have associated the war with the destruction of al-Qaeda and the elimination of transnational terrorism, organizing ourselves around the idea of preventing another 9/11.

The Afghanistan Papers effectively catalog the deeply dysfunctional nature of the war, from its continuously flawed strategy to its bungled execution. Upon release of the papers, certain members of Congress noisily expressed their outrage, as though learning for the first time of our history of failed policies in Afghanistan. This includes Senator Richard Blumenthal, a Vietnam-era veteran infamous for insinuating that he had, in fact, fought in that war as opposed to having simply served during the same time period. He sits on the Senate Armed Services Committee, and takes to Twitter, immediately calling for hearings and writing, "We must end the vicious, lethal cycle of misinformation & unspecified, unsupported strategies."

Such sudden indignation. Do we, the American people, really need an elaborate unearthing of thousands of previously classified documents to tell us that our efforts in Afghanistan have not gone well? Anyone paying the slightest attention to the war can see how it's festered for two decades—the duration alone telling you that it's been a disastrous undertaking. As does this number: 2,461 Americans dead. As well as a bill that comes to over $2 trillion. The *Washington Post* opens its story with the following: "A confidential trove of government documents . . . reveals that senior U.S. officials failed to tell the truth about the war in Afghanistan throughout the 18-year campaign, making rosy pronouncements they knew to be false and hiding unmistakable evidence the war had become unwinnable."

Inherent in this statement is the logic that the American people were misled and *because* they were misled they gave successive administrations their consent to continue prosecuting the war. What is unspoken in this logic is that *if* the American people knew how poorly the war was going, they would've mobilized to end it, much as they mobilized to eventually end the Vietnam War. That mobilization never comes for Afghanistan. This isn't because of a lack of "truth" or of "facts." It is because of a lack of interest.

As Kabul falls, it is disorienting to see Americans newly interested in Afghanistan. Policy makers and military professionals certainly deserve blame for this debacle. And yet the American people share the burden of this blame too. Unlike other systemic social problems that have resulted in the mobilization of average citizens, ending foreign conflicts has so far failed to result in a domestic protest movement. The costs of foreign wars no longer lodge in the American consciousness as something we have to own. This is rooted in how we make war: we pay no war tax and place those costs into our national deficit, having chosen to pass them along to future generations; also, we unquestioningly outsource our national defense to a military caste, largely recruited from the same regions and increasingly from the same families, who bear the burden of these muddled conflicts.

In the run-up to the 2018 midterm elections, Rasmussen placed a poll into the field to see what issues Americans cared about the most. When asked about Afghanistan, 42 percent of Americans couldn't say whether we were still at war there. It's not that they didn't care; they didn't even know. Is it a coincidence that in our history the wars we've decisively won were largely fought by citizen soldiers and a public so inconvenienced by war that it would never abide the cyclical quagmires that have become the signature of today's American foreign policy?

The first part of the *Washington Post*'s series is headlined "At War with the Truth." However, it doesn't tell us who, exactly, is at war with the truth. The inference seems to be that it is the "government," which, as Justice Black wrote in his opinion, "a free and unrestrained press can effectively expose." But what if it's not the government? What if it goes deeper than that? What if it's us, *we the people*, who after two decades of war still lack the resolve to look in the mirror and ask ourselves how we got here and whether we're willing to change so that it never happens again? The free press can expose government duplicity, as it has in the past. But what about societal duplicity? Who will expose that?

THE AFGHANISTAN PAPERS | THE SECRET HISTORY OF THE WAR

AT WAR WITH THE TRUTH

U.S. officials constantly said they were making progress. They were not, confidential documents show, and they knew it.

BY CRAIG WHITLOCK

A confidential trove of government documents obtained by The Washington Post reveals that senior U.S. officials failed to tell the truth about the war in Afghanistan throughout the 18-year campaign, making rosy pronouncements they knew to be false and hiding unmistakable evidence the war had become unwinnable.

The documents were generated by a federal project examining the root failures of the longest armed conflict in U.S. history. They include more than 2,000 pages of previously unpublished notes of interviews with people who played a direct role in the war, from generals and diplomats to aid workers and Afghan officials.

The U.S. government tried to shield the identities of the vast majority of those interviewed for the project and conceal nearly all of their remarks. The Post kept release of the documents under the Freedom of Information Act after a three-year legal battle.

In the interviews, more than 400 insiders offered unrestrained

criticism of what went wrong in Afghanistan and how the United States became mired in nearly two decades of warfare.

With a bluntness rarely expressed in public, the interviews lay bare pent-up complaints, frustrations and confessions, along with second-guessing and backbiting.

"We were devoid of a fundamental understanding of Afghanistan — we didn't know what we were doing," Douglas Lute, a three-star Army general who served as the White House's Afghan war czar during the Bush and Obama administrations, told government interviewers in 2015. He added: "What are we trying to do here? We didn't have the foggiest notion of what we were undertaking."

"If the American people knew the magnitude of this dysfunction ... 2,400 lives lost," Lute added,
SEE AFGHANISTAN ON A11

Our friends didn't have to die: Veterans, journalists and experts express shock and familiar frustrations about the report. A16

LESSONS LEARNED RECORD OF INTERVIEW

After a three-year legal battle, The Post won release of more than 2,000 pages of U.S. government interview records recording candid accounts — from generals, ambassadors, diplomats and other war insiders — of U.S. failures in Afghanistan. This exclusive Post report is the first of six based on revelations in the documents.

🖥 Explore the documents at wapo.st/afghanistan-papers

TOP: Afghan soldiers carry a wounded comrade to a U.S. medevac helicopter after a Taliban ambush in Kunar province, in northeastern Afghanistan, in 2010.

SPIN	STRATEGY	NATION-BUILDING	CORRUPTION	SECURITY FORCES	OPIUM
Today: How officials misrepresented 18 years of setbacks.	**Wednesday:** Unclear objectives dogged the war from the start.	**Thursday:** The United States has exerted billions on reconstruction efforts.	**Friday:** How U.S. officials allowed graft and thievery to thrive.	**Saturday:** Creating a force proved impossible.	**Sunday:** Poppy farming exploited despite attempts to curb it.

1996 memo details Warren's work on side of corporations

BY ANNIE LINSKEY AND MATT VISER

The memo from then-Professor Elizabeth Warren was written on Harvard Law School letterhead, a symbol of gravitas for a scholar renowned as a champion for consumers victimized by predatory banks and other big business.

But on this occasion, Warren was not arguing on behalf of vulnerable families, nor was she offering the sort of stinging rebuke of corporate greed that would later define her political

career. Rather, Warren was representing a large development company that was trying to avoid having to clean up a toxic waste site.

The memo, which Warren wrote in 1996, used legalistic and often dense language to argue that businesses faced the "risk of the unknown" from a growing threat of lawsuits, and that defended the company's right to "maximize its returns to its on-

Battling fundraising: Candidate promises more transparency. A4

SEE WARREN ON A4

PAUL A. VOLCKER 1927-2019

Fed chairman left deep imprint

Helped U.S. go off gold standard, curbed inflation with high interest rates

BY NEIL IRWIN

Paul A. Volcker, a hard-nosed economic statesman who as chairman of the Federal Reserve from 1979 to 1987 shocked the U.S. economy out of a cycle of inflation and malaise and so set the stage for a generation of prosperity, died Dec. 8 at his home in Manhattan. He was 92.

The cause was complications from prostate cancer, said his daughter, Janice Zima.

With influence that spanned five decades and seven presidents, Mr. Volcker left as deep an imprint on speculative activity by banks that would become known as the "Volcker Rule."

Mr. Volcker was a giant of a man, standing 6-foot-7,

Paul A. Volcker

As a senior Treasury official in the 1960s and early '70s, he advised President Richard M. Nixon on taking the United States off the gold standard. At the Fed, he was arguably the second-most-powerful person in the country.

As an adviser to presidential candidate Barack Obama, he gave the young senator credibility. He later counseled him as president on his response to the 2008 financial crisis and proposed a key restriction on

SEE VOLCKER ON A18

Trump is called 'a risk to' U.S.

DEMOCRATS OUTLINE IMPEACHMENT CASE

Republicans defend him, disrupt Judiciary hearing

BY RACHAEL BADE, MIKE DeBONIS, ELISE VIEBECK AND TOLUSE OLORUNNIPA

House Democrats began to lay the groundwork for articles of impeachment Monday, instigating President Trump as a danger to the country during a contentious hearing that foreshadowed a party-line vote on charges that could include abuse of power, obstruction of justice and obstruction of Congress.

Over the vociferous and at times disruptive objections of Republicans, Democratic lawmakers marched forward with their public case for impeaching Trump, a process that could reach a pivotal stage later this week with a historic committee vote.

Describing Trump as a "continuing risk to the country," House Judiciary Committee Chairman Jerrold Nadler (D-N.Y.) forcefully accused the president of using his office to pressure Ukraine to launch political investigations and then trying to block Congress from investigating him.

"President Trump put himself before country," he said. "The president welcomed foreign interference in our election in 2016, he demanded it in 2020, and then he got caught."

Republicans on the committee sought to vigorously defend Trump, using parliamentary maneuvers, process complaints and
SEE IMPEACHMENT ON A6

'Personal' time: Inside Trump war travels with "shadow" outline. A7

FBI probe of Trump not biased, report says

But inspector general finds other 'failures' in handling of investigation

BY DEVLIN BARRETT, MATT ZAPOTOSKY, KAROUN DEMIRJIAN AND ELLEN NAKASHIMA

A Justice Department inspector general's report examining the FBI investigation of President Trump's 2016 campaign rebutted conservatives' accusations that top FBI officials were driven by political bias to illegally spy on Trump advisers but also found broad and "serious performance failures" regarding major changes.

The 434-page report issued Monday by Justice Department Inspector General Michael Horowitz concluded that the FBI had an "authorized purpose" when it initiated its investigation, known as Crossfire Hurricane, into the Trump campaign. In doing so, Horowitz implicitly rejected assertions by the president and fellow Republicans that the case was launched out of political animus or that the FBI broke its own rules on using informants.

As the probe went on and the FBI sought court approval to
SEE REPORT ON A8

Trusted tip: With investigation, FBI hit it received a "tipping point." A8

CONTENT © 2019
The Washington Post · Year 142, No. 11

Ever since I returned from our wars in Iraq and Afghanistan, people have, from time to time, casually asked me what combat is like. Typically, I'll direct them to films like *Full Metal Jacket* and *Black Hawk Down*, which, in my opinion, do a pretty good job of capturing something of the experience. Then, in 2021, I begin to recommend another film.

After the January 6 storming of the Capitol, a video began circulating among veterans I know. It is a roughly forty-minute continuous shot that moves from the breach on the western staircase of the Capitol to the shooting of one of the rioters, Ashli Babbitt, an Air Force veteran, outside the Speaker's Lobby. When sending it, many of the veterans asked, "What does this remind you of?" I watched with my heart in my throat—the exhilaration of the participants, the chaos of a historic event playing out around you, the violence and latent presence of madness; it reminded me of combat.

I say this not to draw a political equivalency between insurrectionists and men and women in uniform, but rather to place a focus on the level of insanity witnessed that day. Anyone who has been to war can tell you that no matter how honorably it is conducted, it is an exercise in collective insanity, where norms of civilized behavior melt away as you engage in the act of state-sanctioned killing.

The video I watched was made by a young man identifying himself as John Sullivan, who goes by the name Jayden X online. His commentary runs throughout the video. After breaching the first line of barricades, he says breathlessly, "I can't believe this is reality! We accomplished this shit! We did this shit together!" And then, "This is fucking history!" That sense of being part of history and the attendant thrill in Sullivan's voice is certainly something that I experienced in combat.

I remember the first night of the Battle of Fallujah—thousands of Marines advancing into the city, jets swarming overhead and dropping their ground-shaking ordnance, and the knowledge that I was part of something that, for a moment, held the entire world in its thrall. Or flying into the Zerkoh Valley, blacked out in helicopters next to Willy and Super Dave, surrounded by those who were also a part of this. *We did this together.* Yes, we certainly did, but we didn't yet know the full implications of what we had done and how it would echo in our own lives and the lives of others for years and decades to come. Violence has a long tail.

Within minutes of the first breach, the crowd pours into the Capitol. On entering an opulent conference room, Sullivan asks himself, "What reality is this?" Then, along with a crowd, he rushes into the Rotunda, and his advance is stalled as if he has hit an invisible wall. He and others are stupefied by what they see: the gilded dome above their heads, the statuary and paintings along the walls. While Trump supporters meander around him, he shouts, "What is this? What is *life?*" A woman, who has been filming him as he is recording her, stops and says, "I'll give you your hug now." They embrace and congratulate each other. Sullivan tells her to watch his YouTube channel, and she says, "You weren't recording, were you?" and he assures her that he'll delete their exchange.

Throughout the video, the elation of the insurrectionists is juxtaposed with the horror of the Capitol Police officers, who know they're overwhelmed and continually seem to be falling back. This vacillation—between horror and ecstasy, not only within groups but also within individuals—attends the madness in every war, and it is the defining characteristic of this video.

Within minutes, Sullivan has pushed to the head of the crowd, which is closing in on the main legislative chambers. When they approach locked doors, he is quick to volunteer his knife to pry them open (though it is never used). Eventually, the crowd stalls at a bank of glass-paneled doors marked "Speaker's Lobby." Law enforcement has barricaded the corridor with office chairs and desks. Sullivan urges the police officers to step away, warning them that they're only going to get hurt. As the crowd continues to break sections of the glass, Sullivan sees an officer aiming a pistol at the mob from the other side of the doors. He shouts, "There's a gun!"

For fourteen seconds, his camera holds steady on the gun aimed at the rioters. He doesn't run away or push anyone else away. He simply repeats, "There's a gun!" over and over. It's as if the experience has left him unclear whether this is real or a dream, unable to imagine he might be the one about to get shot. Violence, up close, is surreal. Your mind struggles to comprehend its own fracturing, and so the response to the most threatening forms of terror often *isn't* terror. It's stupefaction, wonder, a sense of "wow, look at that."

Sullivan survives this altercation. But Ashli Babbitt does not. When a glass panel on one of the doors is completely shattered, she climbs through and is shot in the neck, collapsing backward onto the floor. The video is graphic, and Sullivan is right there. His camera finally turns off as she lies dying at his feet.

After watching the video, I felt depleted. Americans have, each in our own way, tried to make sense of what happened that day, with everything from impeachment proceedings to condemnations to a congressional commission. However, a solely political response to what occurred is insufficient. It requires an emotional understanding as well.

In a follow-up video, Sullivan, who says he believes that "Black lives matter" but is not a part of a Black Lives Matter organization, explains that he also believes in "recording these situations and allowing people to see it for what it is." Yet it is hard to square his professed politics with his actions in the video, in which he is clearly a participant, trying to help rioters penetrate more deeply into the Capitol. I only bring up Sullivan's stated beliefs to show that there is a political incoherence that characterizes events like this. It's the same in war.

Sullivan's political rationale for why he stormed the Capitol lasts twenty minutes and is opaque at best. But his emotional rationale is crystal clear: "Who doesn't want to be there for the action, right? Who doesn't want to see a bunch of Trump supporters just fuck up the Capitol? . . . That's why you watched it. You watched it as an action movie." This brand of nihilism—destruction for the sake of spectacle— is ubiquitous in war.

On my way home from my first combat deployment in Iraq, I spent the night in a transient barracks. Graffiti by those returning from combat littered the plywood walls. Scrawled in one corner in black Sharpie was a quote by Friedrich Nietzsche: "Anyone who fights with monsters should take care that he does not in the process become a monster. And if you gaze for long enough into an abyss, the abyss gazes back into you." I was twenty-four years old, and those words felt like a revelation. Reading them seemed like a first step in the process of understanding not only what I'd been through but also this distinctly human practice: war.

Watching the storming of the Capitol felt similar to reading those words, not only in that I was understanding some new shade of human darkness, but also that I was gazing at something that, like war, had a certain inexplicable quality: it was gazing right back into me.

SCENE II

Arlington National Cemetery, 2008

Tubes died in the summer. His funeral took place in the fall, in October, the same month we came home. His family had waited for us to return before holding the service. They sat clustered at his graveside while those of us who'd fought alongside him stood in our dress blue uniforms in loosely ordered ranks intermingled among the headstones of Section 60, which contained the Iraq and Afghanistan war dead. Those of us gathered at Arlington had watched as, over previous years, our friends had filled out this section. A few of us would go on to fill out the section ourselves in the years to come. But that day we'd shown up for Tubes and so kept such thoughts to ourselves, or waited until later—that night over a drink, perhaps—to speak them.

Tubes's two young sons were there. His wife was there too. And many of us—myself included—who'd found our courage in other situations, struggled to find the courage to speak more than a few limp words of condolence to them. A friend of mine, Kirk, had also come. A successful Washington, D.C.–based businessman, he centered his philanthropic efforts around providing scholarships for the children of fallen service members. His philanthropy had already made a financial commitment to ensure the education of Tubes's boys. He'd wanted to attend the funeral to show his respect. He'd only just met Tubes's family and hardly knew anyone else at the service, so he stood with me.

A chaplain delivered remarks, his prayers muffled by the airplanes landing two miles away at Reagan National Airport. A detail of five riflemen fired a volley into the air, a final salute. A bugler blew taps. The flag was silently folded and passed to the family. In less than twenty minutes, it was over. The burial detail marched out of Section 60, leaving the family to linger graveside for as long as they liked. I thanked Kirk for coming and shook his hand before wandering off with the likes of Willy and Super Dave and a few others, to pay our respects to other friends who were buried here. As we filtered out among the gravestones, about fifty yards away, I noticed a navy officer who'd been watching the ceremony. His wife stood beside him, the two of them arm in arm. From the glint of heavy gold braid on his sleeve, I could tell he was a very senior officer. But I couldn't tell exactly who he was—that is, until I stepped a bit closer.

Throughout the ceremony, Admiral Mike Mullen, the chairman of the Joint Chiefs of Staff, had been watching at a distance so as not to draw any attention to himself. He was then America's senior-most military officer, responsible for the war Tubes had died fighting. He'd never met Tubes, never met any of us, yet he'd carved out the time to

attend the funeral with his wife. He did so without any fanfare, so their presence wouldn't distract from the ceremony. It was just the two of them. Before I could point out the admiral to anyone else, he was gone. A black SUV idling nearby whisked him back to his office in the Pentagon.

A few days later, I received a phone call from Kirk. Ostensibly, he wanted to update me on the scholarships for Tubes's boys, though the real purpose of his call was slightly different. Eventually, he got around to saying, "I've done this work on behalf of gold star families for a while, but I've never attended a funeral. That will stick with me for a long time."

I told him that I appreciated his call and was grateful for the work he was doing to help the family. I then asked him if he'd noticed the navy officer who'd been standing off to the side. Kirk had noticed, and said he'd been wondering who that was. I explained that it'd been

Admiral Mullen and how seeing him there was what would stick with me. Kirk added, "You know what else is going to stick with me? Watching you guys wander off to the other headstones after the funeral. I don't know why, but it hadn't occurred to me that Tubes wouldn't be the only friend of yours buried at Arlington."

"Yeah . . . well . . ." And suddenly I didn't know quite what to say, so I simply settled on "Seven years is a long time to be fighting a war."

SCENE III

A stone house, Puglia

We've arrived at the seaside. We've been gone a week and have a week left on our trip. We'll spend that time here. The plan is to swim, to eat, to rest, to have fun as a family at summer's end. The collapse of Kabul continues in the background, particularly as the last week of our trip coincides with the last week that HKIA will remain in US hands. The situation at the airport is becoming more desperate as the window for evacuation narrows. Everyone I know with any connection to Afghanistan—from soldiers to journalists to aid workers—is trying to help in the evacuation. Signal and WhatsApp group chats with titles like "3rd Flight Funding," "HLZ Extract," and "North Gate Access for Safi" clutter my phone. I can't keep up with the volume of messages or the participants involved, who in most cases I hardly know.

The day after Shah makes it through the North Gate, I find myself on the phone with Sherrie Westin, the president of Sesame Workshop, the nonprofit behind *Sesame Street*. A mutual friend has put us in touch. She's trying to evacuate twenty-three puppeteers from *Baghch-e-Simsin*, the Afghan *Sesame Street*. That show, which premiered in 2016, introduced the first Afghan Muppet, a six-year-old girl named Zari, which means "shimmering" in Dari. Before she was taken off the air, Zari the Muppet loved going to school and spoke about it often. The show became the most-watched TV program among children in Afghanistan. Eighty-one percent of children aged three to seven saw Zari on television. As did the Taliban. Which is why Sherrie Westin is determined to get her puppeteers out of Kabul.

Sherrie is relentlessly upbeat in her efforts. Even though I don't have great news for her, she is determined, whereas I must sound a bit worn out. At one point, I tell her that the door is closing on these flights, that most people aren't going to get out, that, in fact, the majority of people are going to be left behind. What I don't say—but rather imply—is that getting only a few people out feels futile when placed against the larger need. After that conversation, she sends me an email linking to an article on a self-help website. With some skepticism, I click the link. It takes me to the following story, a parable:

Once upon a time, there was an old man who used to go to the ocean for exercise. One day, the old man was walking along a beach that was littered with thousands of starfish that had been washed ashore by the high tide. As he walked he came upon a young boy who was eagerly throwing the starfish back into the ocean, one by one.

Puzzled, the man looked at the boy and asked what he was doing.

The young boy paused, looked up, and replied, "Throwing starfish into the ocean. The tide has washed them up onto the beach and they can't return to the sea by themselves. When the sun gets high, they will die, unless I throw them back into the water."

The old man replied, "But there must be tens of thousands of starfish on this beach. I'm afraid you won't really be able to make much of a difference."

The boy bent down, picked up yet another starfish, and threw it as far as he could into the ocean. Then he turned, smiled, and said, "I made a difference for that one."

The cynic in me wants to dismiss this homespun wisdom, but after a morning spent with my own children—on a beach like the one in this story, no less—I find that difficult to do. Sherrie's message isn't the only one waiting for me after a few hours away from my phone. Ian has been in touch. He has another group he's trying to get out. I also have an email from a friend who leads a Washington, D.C.–based center for the promotion of democracy. His name is Hardy, and his email begins formally, "I hope this message finds you and your family well," and I can imagine the many people he has likely sent it to. The email goes on to outline the plight of a dozen Afghans he's trying to help, a group of translators and democratic activists trapped in Kabul. Attached to the email is a list of their names. The email ends, "Thank you very much for any help you are able to provide in this case."

I call Ian. I then call Hardy. Both groups, twenty-nine people in all, are at the airport right now, waiting outside and not far from one another. If we move quickly, they could link up. With a little luck, we might have an opportunity to get everyone out. I send a message to Richardella, to see if his Marines can help us one more time: *I've got a group trying to get through Abbey Gate (just got notified). See attached. Is this possible right now?*

Then I wait for a reply.

While I'm waiting, I receive another message from Sherrie. Her persistence has paid off. Her puppeteers are inside the airport. They'll fly out tonight.

SCENE IV

Korengal Valley, Kunar Province, 2009

I was back in Afghanistan a year after Tubes's funeral, though not as a Marine. I was now a paramilitary officer working for the CIA. My first mission with the organization was against a top-ten al-Qaeda target. I had been deployed in my new job—one Jack had helped me get—for a total of two days. On this mission it was our CTPT and a handful of members from SEAL Team Six. Our plan was to conduct a raid to capture or kill our target, who was coming across the border from Pakistan for a meeting in the Korengal Valley.

The night was moonless as we slipped into the valley. The seventy-odd members of our raid force hiked under night-vision goggles for a couple of hours, taking on hundreds of feet of elevation in silence until we arrived at a village on a rocky outcropping where the meeting was being held. As surveillance and strike aircraft orbited the starry sky, a subset of our force sprinted toward the house where an informant had told us the target was staying. There was a brief and sharp gunfight; none of our men were hurt, and several of our adversaries were killed. But the target was taken alive. Then we slipped out of the valley as expeditiously as we had arrived. By early morning, we had made it safely to the nearest US Army outpost, where our prisoner would soon be transferred to Bagram Air Base.

The sun was breaking over the jagged ridgeline as we filled out the paperwork transferring custody. The mood among our raid force, which had remained tense all night, suddenly eased. We lounged in a small dirt parking lot, helmets off, laughing and recounting the details of our mission. A convoy would soon arrive to usher us back to our base, where we would get some much-needed rest and a decent meal. We would then await our next target, continuing what was proving to be a successful campaign to decapitate al-Qaeda's leadership. We were feeling, in short, victorious.

While we waited, a column of scraggly American soldiers, little older than teenagers, filed past. They lived at the outpost, and their plight was well-known to us. For the past several years, they had been waging a quixotic and largely unsuccessful counterinsurgency campaign in the valley. Many of their friends had been killed there, and their expressions were haggard, a mix of defeat and defiance. Our triumphant banter must have sounded to them like a foreign language. They gave us hard, resentful looks, treating us as interlopers. It occurred to me that although our counterterrorism unit was standing on the same battlefield as these soldiers, we were in fact fighting in two very different wars.

At a joint session of Congress on September 20, 2001, President Bush announced what was then a new type of war, a "war on terror." He laid out its terms: "We will direct every resource at our command—every means of diplomacy, every tool of intelligence, every instrument of law enforcement, every financial influence, and every necessary weapon of war—to the disruption and to the defeat of the global terror network." Then he described what that defeat might look like: "We will starve terrorists of funding, turn them one against another, drive them from place to place until there is no refuge or no rest."

If Bush's words outlined the essential objectives of the global war on terror, twenty years later the United States has largely achieved them. Osama bin Laden is dead. The surviving core members of al-Qaeda are dispersed and weak. Bin Laden's successor, Ayman al-Zawahiri, communicates only through rare propaganda releases, and al-Qaeda's most powerful offshoot, the Islamic State, has seen its territorial holdings dwindle to insignificance in Iraq and Syria. Our calamitous withdrawal from Afghanistan could undermine these accomplishments, but that is where the United States stands as Kabul falls.

Most important of these accomplishments is our success in securing the homeland. If someone had told Americans in the weeks after 9/11—as they navigated anthrax attacks on the Capitol, a plunging stock market, and predictions of the demise of mass travel—that the US military and US intelligence agencies would successfully shield the country from another major terrorist attack for the next twenty years, they would have had trouble believing it. Since 9/11, the United States has suffered, on average, six deaths per year due to jihadi terrorism. (To put this in perspective, in 2019, an average of thirty-eight Americans died every day from overdoses involving prescription opioids.) If the goal of the global war on terrorism has been to prevent significant acts of terrorism, then the war has succeeded.

But at what cost? Like that night in the Korengal, can success and failure coexist on the same battlefield? Can the United States claim to have won the war on terror while having simultaneously lost (or at least not won) the wars in Afghanistan and Iraq?

Let's start by framing the discussion of cost around blood and treasure. Every war the United States has fought, beginning with the American Revolution, has required an economic model to sustain it with sufficient bodies and cash. Like its predecessors, the war on terror came with its own model: as discussed, the war was fought by an all-volunteer military and paid for largely through deficit spending. It should be no surprise that this model, which by design anesthetized a majority of Americans to the costs of conflict, delivered us our longest war.

This model has also had a profound effect on American democracy, one that is only being fully understood twenty years later. Today, with a ballooning national deficit paired with inflation, it is worth noting that the war on terror became one of the earliest and most expensive charges on our national credit card after the balanced budgets of the 1990s; 2001 marked the last year that the federal budget passed by Congress resulted in a surplus. Funding the war through deficit spending allowed it to fester through successive administrations with hardly a single politician ever mentioning the idea of a war tax. Meanwhile, other forms of spending—from financial bailouts to health care and, most recently, a pandemic recovery stimulus package—generate breathless debate.

If deficit spending has anesthetized the American people to the fiscal cost of the war on terror, technological and social changes have numbed them to its human cost. The use of drone aircraft and other platforms has facilitated the growing automation of combat, which allows the US military to kill remotely. This development has further distanced Americans from the grim costs of war, whether they be deaths of US troops or those of foreign civilians. Meanwhile, the absence of a draft has allowed the US government to outsource its wars to a military caste, an increasingly self-segregated portion of society, opening up a yawning civil-military divide as profound as American society has ever known.

In 2020, in response to nationwide civil unrest, Americans finally had the chance to meet their military firsthand, as both active-duty and National Guard troops were deployed in large numbers throughout the country. Americans also got to hear from the military's retired leadership, as a bevy of flag officers—both on the right and the left—weighed in on domestic political matters in unprecedented ways. They spoke on television, wrote editorials that denounced one party or the other, and signed their names to letters on everything from the provenance of a suspicious laptop connected to the Democratic nominee's son to the integrity of the presidential election itself.

For now, the military remains one of the most trusted institutions in the United States and one of the few that the public sees as having no overt political bias. How long will this trust last under existing political conditions? As partisanship taints every facet of American life, it would seem to be only a matter of time before that infection spreads to the US military. What then? From Caesar's Rome to Napoléon's France, history shows that when a republic couples a large standing military with dysfunctional domestic politics, democracy doesn't last long. The United States today meets both conditions. Historically, this has invited the type of political crisis that leads to military involvement (or even intervention) in domestic politics. The wide divide between the military and the citizens it serves is yet another inheritance from the war on terror.

Although it may seem odd to separate the wars in Afghanistan and Iraq from the war on terror, it is worth remembering that immediately after 9/11, the wholesale invasion and occupation of either country was hardly a fait accompli. It is not difficult to imagine a more limited counterterrorism campaign in Afghanistan that might have brought bin Laden to justice or a strategy to contain Saddam Hussein's Iraq that would not have involved a full-scale US invasion. The long, costly counterinsurgency campaigns that followed in each country were wars of choice. Both proved to be major missteps when it came to achieving the twin goals of bringing the perpetrators of 9/11 to justice and securing the homeland.

What has made the war on terror different from other wars is that victory has never been based on achieving a positive outcome; the goal has been to prevent a negative one. In this war, victory doesn't come when you destroy your adversary's army or seize its capital. It occurs when something does not happen. How, then, do you declare victory? How do you prove a negative? After 9/11, it was almost as though American strategists, unable to conceptualize a war that could be won only by not allowing a certain set of events to replicate themselves, felt forced to create a war that conformed to more conventional conceptions of conflict. The wars in Afghanistan and Iraq represented a familiar type of war, with an invasion to topple a tyrannical government and liberate a people, followed by a long occupation and counterinsurgency campaigns.

In addition to blood and treasure, there is another metric by which the war on terror can be judged: opportunity cost. The COVID-19 pandemic has revealed the depths of American political dysfunction and has hinted at the dangers of a civil-military divide. Perhaps even more important from a national security perspective, it has also brought the United States' complex relationship with China into stark relief. For the past two decades, while Washington was repurposing the US military to engage in massive counterinsurgency campaigns and precision counterterrorism operations, Beijing was busy building a military to fight and defeat a peer-level competitor.

Today, the Chinese navy is the largest in the world. It boasts 350 commissioned warships to the US Navy's roughly 290. Although US ships generally outclass their Chinese counterparts, it now seems inevitable that the two countries' militaries will one day reach parity. China has spent twenty years building a chain of artificial islands throughout the South China Sea that can effectively serve as a defensive line of unsinkable aircraft carriers. Culturally, China has become more militaristic, producing hypernationalist content such as the *Wolf Warrior* action movies. In the first, a former US Navy SEAL plays the archvillain. The sequel, released in 2017, became the highest-grossing film in Chinese box-office history; that is, until 2021, when *The Battle at Lake Changjin* beat its record.

That film is about a Chinese victory over US forces in the Korean War. Clearly, Beijing has no qualms about framing Washington as an antagonist. After Kabul falls, China is one of the first nations to recognize the newly formed Taliban government.

China isn't the only country that has taken advantage of a preoccupied United States. In the past two decades, Russia has expanded its territory into Crimea and backed a separatist movement that culminated in an invasion of Ukraine; Iran has backed proxies in Afghanistan, Iraq, and Syria; and North Korea has acquired nuclear weapons. After the century opened with 9/11, conventional wisdom had it that nonstate actors would prove to be the greatest threat to US national security. This prediction came true, but not in the way most people anticipated. Nonstate actors have compromised US national security not by attacking the United States but by diverting its attention away from state actors. It is these classic antagonists—China, Russia, Iran, and North Korea—that have expanded their capabilities and antipathies in the face of a distracted United States.

How imminent is the threat from these states? When it comes to legacy military platforms—aircraft carriers, tanks, fighter planes—the United States continues to enjoy a healthy technological dominance over its near-peer competitors. But its preferred platforms might not be the right ones. Long-range, land-based cruise missiles could render large aircraft carriers obsolete. Advances in cyber offense could make tech-reliant fighter aircraft too vulnerable to fly. The greatest minds in the US military have now, finally, turned their attention to these concerns, with the US Marine Corps, for example, shifting its entire strategic focus to a potential conflict with China. But it may be too late.

After two decades, the United States also suffers from war fatigue. Even though an all-volunteer military and the lack of a war tax have exempted most Americans from shouldering the burdens of war, that fatigue has still manifested. Under four presidents, the American people at first celebrated and then endured the endless wars playing in the background of their lives. Gradually, the national mood soured, and adversaries have taken notice. Americans' fatigue—and rival countries' recognition of it—has limited the United States' strategic options. As a result, presidents have adopted policies of inaction, and American credibility has eroded.

This dynamic played out most starkly in Syria, in the aftermath of the August 2013 sarin gas attack in Ghouta. When Syrian president Bashar al-Assad crossed President Obama's stated red line by using chemical weapons, Obama found that not only was the international community no longer as responsive to an American president's entreaties for the use of force but also that this reluctance appeared in Congress as well. When Obama went to legislators to gain support for a military strike against the Assad regime, he encountered bipartisan war fatigue that mirrored the fatigue of voters, and he called off the attack. The United States' red line had been crossed, without incident or reprisal.

Fatigue may seem like a "soft" cost of the war on terror, but it is a glaring strategic liability. A nation exhausted by war has a difficult time presenting a credible deterrent threat to adversaries. This proved to be true during the Cold War when, at the height of the Vietnam War, in 1968, the Soviets invaded Czechoslovakia, and when, in the war's aftermath, in 1979, the Soviets invaded Afghanistan. Because it was embroiled in a war in the first case and reeling from it in the second, the United States could not credibly deter Soviet military aggression. The United States is in a similar spot today, particularly with regard to China. Not long before Kabul fell, when Americans were asked in a poll whether the United States should defend Taiwan if it were confronted with an invasion by China, 55 percent of respondents said that it should not.

Obviously, if the Chinese undertook such an action, particularly if Americans or the citizens of allied countries were killed in the process, public opinion might change swiftly; nevertheless, the poll suggested that the threshold for the use of force has risen among Americans. US adversaries understand this. It is no coincidence that China, for instance, has felt empowered to infringe on Hong Kong's autonomy and commit brazen human rights abuses against its own minority Uighur population. When American power recedes, other states fill the vacuum.

The war on terror has changed both how the United States sees itself and how it is perceived by the rest of the world. From time to time, people have asked in what ways the war changed me. I have never known how to answer this question because ultimately the war didn't change me; the war made me. It is so deeply ingrained in my psyche that I have a difficult time separating the parts of me that exist because of it from the parts of me that exist despite it. Answering that question is like explaining how a parent or a sibling changed you. When you live with a war—as you would a person—for so long, you come to know it on intimate terms, and it comes to change you in similarly intimate ways.

Today, I have a hard time remembering what the United States used to be like. I forget what it was like to arrive at the airport just twenty minutes before a flight. What it was like to walk through a train station without armed police meandering around the platforms. Or what it was like to believe—particularly in those heady years right after the Cold War—that the United States' version of democracy would remain ascendant for all time and that the world had reached "the end of history."

In much the same way members of the Greatest Generation can recall where they were when the Japanese attacked Pearl Harbor or baby boomers can recall where they were when JFK was shot, my generation's touchstone is where you were on 9/11. Like most of us, I remember the day clearly. But when thinking of that time, the event I return to most often happened two nights before.

I was a college student and had requisitioned the television in my apartment because HBO was premiering a new series, *Band of Brothers*. As an ROTC midshipman, I believed my entire future would be spent as part of a band of brothers. As I settled onto the sofa, that iconic title sequence started: sepia-toned paratroopers falling across the sky en route to liberating Europe, the swelling strings of the nostalgic soundtrack. There wasn't a hint of irony or cynicism anywhere in the series. I can't imagine someone making it today.

As the United States' sensibilities about war—and warriors—have changed over two decades, I have often thought of *Band of Brothers*. It's a good barometer of where the country was before 9/11 and the emotional distance it has traveled since. Today, the United States is different; it is skeptical of its role in the world, more clear-eyed about the costs of war despite only having experienced those costs in predominantly tangential ways. Our appetite to export our ideals abroad is also diminished, particularly as we struggle to uphold those ideals at home—a struggle that was evident in the violence around the 2020 presidential election, the summer of 2020's civil unrest, or even the way the war on terror compromised the country through scandals, from Abu Ghraib prison to Edward Snowden's leaks. A United States in which *Band of Brothers* has near universal appeal is a distant memory.

It is also a reminder that national narratives matter. The day before the United States departed on a twenty-year odyssey in the Middle East, the stories people wanted to hear—or at least the stories Hollywood executives believed they wanted to hear—were the ones in which the Americans were the good guys, liberating the world from tyranny and oppression.

Not long after President Biden announced the US withdrawal from Afghanistan, I was speaking with Jack. He had also fought in the Korengal Valley, but for far longer than I had. He had also hunted down targets, killing or capturing them, as we all did in the war on terror. The idea that we would be remembered as the ones who lost the United States' longest war had lodged bitterly in our minds. To ease the sting of that conclusion, I offered up a counterargument, which was that even though we might have lost the war in Afghanistan, our generation could still claim to have won the war on terror.

Jack was skeptical.

We debated the issue but soon let it drop. The next day, I received an email from him. Being a southerner and a lover of literature, he had sent me the following, from *The Sound and the Fury:*

> No battle is ever won. . . . They are not even fought. The field only reveals to man his own folly and despair, and victory is an illusion of philosophers and fools.

SCENE V

The Pentagon, 2010

I had a pass that allowed me to park my car at the front of the building, next to the secretary's helicopter pad. It was late autumn and unseasonably warm. The sun was shining, the sky a vast mantle of blue. After leaving the Marines, I had traded in the four-wheel-drive SUV that I once drove between gunnery ranges at Camp Lejeune for a soft-top convertible, a navy '88 BMW 3 Series that I now used for my commute into CIA headquarters. My new car was fun and retro; it even had a tape deck that I'd rigged to the jack in my iPhone. Pulling up to the Pentagon, I turned down my music as the military police ran mirrors beneath the chassis of my car before finally handing me a pass to tuck in my windshield and waving me through. I was early to my meeting, so I sat in the driver's seat for a few minutes, staring north across the Potomac River, toward Washington, D.C. Off to my right was Reagan

National Airport. To my left was Arlington National Cemetery. The planes flew from left to right, over the cemetery, into the airport, passing close to the Pentagon.

The flight path reminded me of funerals at Arlington. They always lasted twenty minutes or so, and it was impossible to have a twenty-minute period during the day when at least one airplane didn't fly overhead, drowning out the service. That had happened at Tubes's funeral a couple of years ago as well as every other funeral I'd been to before and since. I couldn't help but find something unsettling in it, a reminder that America wouldn't pause at the loss. Planes needed to land. Commuters needed to commute. Life needed to go on. Because what else could it do? That afternoon, however, Tubes was foremost on my mind as I sat in the parking lot waiting to head inside. He was the reason I was having this meeting.

A couple weeks before, I'd received a phone call from Kirk. He had gone to a charity benefit for veterans in Washington, D.C., where he'd met Admiral Mike Mullen. Kirk had mentioned the work he did funding scholarships for children from gold star families, to include Tubes's family. Kirk thanked the admiral for attending the funeral. When the admiral asked Kirk how he'd come to know the family, my name had come up. A couple of days later, I had an email from a staffer working in the office of the chairman of the Joint Chiefs asking that I come by to see the admiral. I wasn't certain what the purpose of the meeting was, simply that I was asked to come and so certainly would. Which was how I wound up parked in front of the helicopter pad at the Pentagon.

I had, of course, wondered why the admiral wanted to see me. Recently, I'd begun asking myself how much longer I would stay in the wars. A few months before, I'd had my first child, a girl. For nearly eight years, I'd existed in one of three states of being: training for deployment, on deployment, or coming back from deployment. It wasn't that I didn't love the work that I did; in fact, I did love it. I loved it desperately, which complicated how I was feeling as I thought about the progression of my life.

The career of a professional soldier progresses in many ways like that of a professional athlete. If I'd been, say, a football player, my early career in the infantry would be equivalent to playing high school ball. Our team was scrappy, with all different levels of ability. Our equipment was shoddy, often secondhand. And we played in a pure way, for the love of the game and for the honor of our little-known team and often under less-than-ideal conditions. At mid-career, my time in Marine special operations would be the equivalent of college ball. The players were at a higher level. Our team had a reputation, and often we went up against those with equal reputations. Our equipment was new. And we played under better conditions. Sometimes, our games even found their way onto television. Later in my career, my time as a paramilitary officer would be the equivalent of playing in the NFL. Some of the best players in the game were on our team, truly elite athletes with big and sometimes even legendary reputations. And we were now going up against the toughest teams, with the toughest players on their rosters. Our equipment was world-class, state-of-the-art. We were even flown to our games on private, often unmarked jets. Our biggest games became national events. If you won the Super Bowl, who knew, you might even meet the president. Playing for such high stakes is difficult to give up. But ultimately, you are still playing the game, whether it's football or something else. Eventually the question becomes, *Is the game what you want to do for the rest of your life?*

For many of my closest friends, people whom I loved and admired and had long modeled myself after, the answer to that question was an unequivocal *yes*. But I was becoming less certain. And if I didn't want to do this work for the rest of my life, now was the time to leave, while I was still young enough (and still alive) to do something else. Which brought me to this meeting with Admiral Mullen. Why did he want to see me? In the days before our meeting, I'd allowed myself to speculate. Perhaps there was an opening on his staff. Or maybe he wanted to talk with me about a special project within the Department of Defense, something that would serve as a stepping-stone to that *something else* I was beginning to consider. Even then, I knew I was allowing my imagination to run away. But he was an admiral and I ranked as a lowly GS-12 on the government pay scale, so there must be some specific reason I'd been summoned.

It was time to head inside. I was feeling optimistic. I didn't even put the top up on my old convertible as I walked into the Pentagon's imposing front entrance, something I'd never done before despite having once worked in the building. On the other side of a hulking set of double doors, I was met by another heavily armed member of the military police. He sat behind a pane of bulletproof glass wearing a ballistic vest. My name was checked against a list. A phone call was placed. Shortly thereafter, an army lieutenant colonel appeared from down an oak-paneled corridor in her service uniform. A leash of gold braid—the aiguillette that distinguished her as an aide-de-camp— corded its way around her right shoulder. She shuttled me down the corridor, to a waiting room across from the chairman's office. His aide explained that the current meeting was running long but that she'd come retrieve me when they were through. She shut the door behind her and left me in the room, which like the corridor was also oak-paneled and boasted a series of prints, scenes from iconic American battles. My eyes ranged the walls. Minutemen at Lexington. Yankees at Gettysburg. Devil Dogs in the Argonne.

One of the prints was of the Battle of Guadalcanal. While staring at it, a very specific thought entered my mind. It was a snippet of dialogue from *The Thin Red Line*, a book set during that battle. This bit of dialogue wasn't from the book, actually, but from the film adaptation directed by Terrence Malick. It occurs when Lieutenant Colonel Gordon Tall, an ambitious butcher of men played by Nick Nolte, is readying himself for an audience with the general who will decide his fate in the coming battle. Tall thinks to himself in a voice-over, *The closer you are to Caesar, the greater the fear.*

Two shut doors and a corridor separated me from the most powerful military officer in the world, and I was very much feeling that fear. I began my journey into the military at seventeen years old, and that day, as I waited for the admiral, I was thirty. For nearly half my life, I'd existed in a hierarchy whose senior-most military authority was the chairman of the Joint Chiefs of Staff. It was a hierarchy designed for war, which is to say a hierarchy designed both to take and to sacrifice life, which is also to say a very potent hierarchy. Its potency, for those who haven't lived under it, can often be surprising. Hierarchy is all-encompassing in military life because life itself is contingent upon it. In war it is your chain of command, your hierarchy, that determines your fate. Orders are orders. Rank is rank. Ambiguity in the hierarchy isn't tolerated. If two officers of the same rank are standing in a room, whoever was promoted first is senior. If they were promoted on the same day, you check the promotion list from that day to see who sits higher up. Someone is always on top. There is always an authority greater than you. A few months before, when I'd arrived at the CIA as a civilian government employee, I found myself disoriented by the absence of this authority. Or, put differently, I found myself disoriented by how often I was consulted about my own life. *Do the following deployment dates work for you? Are you available to come in this weekend? Make sure you're keeping track of your overtime.*

Such sudden and unfathomable agency.

But old habits die hard. Even though I no longer wore a uniform, Admiral Mullen's supreme position in that hierarchy left me sitting in the waiting room in an anxious haze. Outside in the corridor, doors opened and shut. I could hear the admiral's aides escorting his previous appointment out of his office. Clearly, they had an elaborate system in place so that each appointment would occur discreetly. A moment later, the aide opened the door. "The chairman is ready for you."

He was, when I entered his office, doing something entirely unexpected. His back was toward me and he was checking his email. It never occurred to me that someone of his rank actually wrote emails or engaged in any other pedestrian administrative task. I guess my subconscious always imagined him and the other four-star demigods who presided over our wars and lives issuing edicts to an attentive staff who transcribed them to email. But here he was, clearing his inbox as his aide announced me at the door. He answered, "One second," drawing out the words as he registered a few final keystrokes before sending whatever message he was composing into the ether. He then swiveled around in his chair. He stood and crossed the room with his hand extended. "Elliot," he said. "Thank you for coming." We shook and he gestured to a sofa opposite from the leather tufted chair where he sat. As a steward served refreshments, the admiral was casual, at ease, a serious man but not self-serious. He asked if I'd had any trouble getting here. He asked where I lived in Washington. He wanted to know exactly when I'd left the Marine Corps. His legs were crossed casually one over the other. He didn't wear his dress uniform, the one I'd seen him in before, but rather his working khakis. His four-star insignia hardly fit on the collar, as if no one had his rank in mind when they'd designed the uniform.

The admiral was quick to ask about my work with the CTPTs. He wanted to know how they measured up versus the Afghan army commandos I'd advised with the Marines. We talked about the Pakistani border and the challenge it posed to our counterinsurgency in Afghanistan. These were, of course, all topics he kept readily abreast of from a variety of sources, to include the intelligence agency where I now worked. Which is to say our conversation on these topics felt pro forma, like a bit of preliminary chitchat. These weren't the reasons the admiral had summoned me. I was, at this moment, wondering if perhaps he was going to reveal that reason, if maybe he was going to explain the special task he needed my help with, or the unexpected opportunity that might change the trajectory of my life and provide a transition out of these wars.

But he didn't. An awkward beat of silence passed between us. At which point I decided to mention the only agenda item I'd arrived with that day. I wanted to thank him for attending Tubes's funeral two years before. When I explained how meaningful it'd been to see him there, he quickly dismissed any fuss I might make over the gesture. He was, in fact, so dismissive that for a moment I wondered if he even remembered the funeral. Which led me to a separate and obvious conclusion: perhaps he had attended so many funerals at Arlington that it was difficult for him to differentiate one from another. Was he standing so far away that day because he hadn't wanted his presence to dominate the ceremony? Or was it that he, himself, needed that distance? If he'd decided to make a point of attending all these funerals, was their cumulative weight too great for him if, in every case, he elected to stand graveside with the family?

Then he asked me something unexpected. "Are you all right?"

I glanced down at my refreshments: the coffee, the cookies, the glass of water. "Yes," I said. "Fine, thank you."

But he asked again, more earnestly, "Are you all right?" adding, "It sounds like you've been through a lot these past years and are still deploying quite a bit. I asked you here because it's helpful for me to have a sense of how you and those like you are doing. How are all of you holding up?"

I told him that I was fine.

Our audience finished shortly thereafter. I stepped outside and climbed into my car. When I pulled out from the Pentagon, the military police stopped me at the gate. I lowered my music. They asked that I return my parking pass.

SCENE VI

A stone house, Puglia

It is night. Lieutenant Colonel Richardella is still at the North Gate. Two groups—one helped by Hardy and the other helped by Ian—are trying to link up at the Abbey Gate, which is on the opposite side of the airport. *Team,* writes Richardella, *I just added my recon company commander, Ryan, and platoon sergeant, Marti. They will assist in snatching guys up at the Abbey Gate.*

The lead person on the ground is an Afghan from Hardy's group. His name is Ahmad. To distinguish himself in the crowd, he is wearing a scarf, do-rag style, on his head. The scarf is turquoise, or what is also called Afghan blue. I post a photograph of him in the chat.

Marti responds to my photograph with one of his own, taken from his vantage at the Abbey Gate. A stone wall abuts a sewage canal. Hundreds of Afghans, mostly men, sit on the wall. A few carry bags; most

do not. They have only the clothes on their backs. Some have waded into the canal, which serves as a barrier into the airport. The photograph was taken with a flash, which reflects in the eyes of some of the men. This makes them look like animals, like cats, or any other startled nocturnal creature. But a closer inspection of the photo reveals it's not the flash that creates this dehumanizing effect, but the desperate circumstances at the airport. Behind them, ringed with concertina wire, is a guard tower. This is part of the security perimeter at the Abbey Gate.

Marti writes, *I have the majority of my teams tasked at the moment. I will have a team there mid afternoon tomorrow. If you can get them to pre-position by this tower, we will get them.*

When I thank Marti for the help, he apologizes that he can't get a team there sooner. His platoon has been busy. He posts to the chat a handwritten list of the groups they have ushered into HKIA over the past several days, with the caption *Closed cases*, as well as the distinct operational name the Marines had assigned to each of those cases— names like *Ladder Time*, 40 pax; *The French Are Coming*, 266 pax; *It Takes a Village*, 134 pax; *Gandalf Support*, 28 pax; *Shits Creek*, 6 pax; *You're Killin' Me SOFLE*, 350 pax; *UN-Fun*, 125 pax; *Shits Creek 2*, 39 pax; *Terpo Tastic*, 7 pax; to name but a few.

Marti posts two other photographs into the chat, as well as the following instructions: *Give your group's senior guy this tasking. When he sees the Marines with the number on their helmets that look like this, and wearing digital green frog cammies, to calmly enter the canal, and make their way to them and pass them the code word the POC from my platoon will give them.* The first photograph that follows shows a Marine wearing the aforementioned green uniform, his arms bowed out from his sides and his palms turned flat as though he's an action figure posed inside plastic packaging. The other photo is of a low-profile ballistic helmet, of the type typically worn by special operations forces, including recon Marines.

It is now late, after midnight. Ian is on the East Coast, where it's still early evening. I need to get some sleep and so ask him if he can run point on coordinating with Ahmad and the others so that they're ready to enter the Abbey Gate tomorrow at noon, Afghan time. Before heading to bed, I check my email, which includes a forwarded message

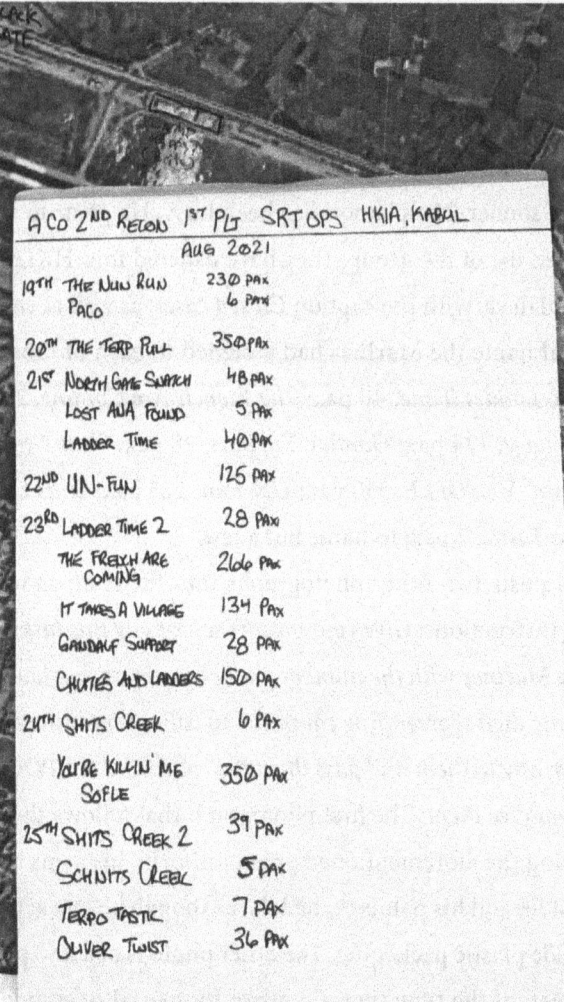

A Co 2ND RECON 1ST PLT SRT OPS HKIA, KABUL

AUG 2021

19TH THE NUN RUN — 230 PAX
PACO — 6 PAX

20TH THE TERP PULL — 350 PAX

21ST NORTH GATE SNATCH — 48 PAX
LOST ANA FOUND — 5 PAX
LADDER TIME — 40 PAX

22ND UN-FUN — 125 PAX

23RD LADDER TIME 2 — 28 PAX
THE FRENCH ARE COMING — 266 PAX
IT TAKES A VILLAGE — 134 PAX
GANDALF SUPPORT — 28 PAX
CHUTES AND LADDERS — 150 PAX

24TH SHITS CREEK — 6 PAX
YOU'RE KILLIN' ME SOFIE — 350 PAX

25TH SHITS CREEK 2 — 39 PAX
SCHNITS CREEK — 5 PAX
TERPO TASTIC — 7 PAX
OLIVER TWIST — 36 PAX

.....WGS-84
.....20 Apr 2021

from Admiral Mullen's wife to Sherrie Westin. The admiral, now re-tired, is trying to evacuate a family in which the father used to work at the US embassy. But progress has proven slow. If the former chairman of the Joint Chiefs is struggling to get someone flown out of HKIA, that doesn't bode well for us. Eventually, I fall asleep.

When I wake up a few hours later, it's to a stream of text messages between Ian, Hardy, and Ahmad. They have consolidated several groups in the vicinity of the Abbey Gate. They exchange rosters, adding the names of those who've met up with Ahmad and deleting the names of those who've given up trying. In war, a truism is that the simple is difficult and the difficult is impossible. Coordinating these evacua-tions lies somewhere between the simple and the difficult. Repeatedly in the text chain we run through how the evacuation will work. Hardy goes so far as to spell it out by the numbers, so everyone understands what they're to do: *Okay, here's my write up of the sequence of events for evac. Please advise/correct this as needed. As I understand it, the se-quence is: 1. At some point Marines will reach out to Ahmad at this number. Note: I have communicated this already to Ahmad. He has saved the Marines number in his phone. 2. Marines emerge from HKIA. 3. Ahmad will be on lookout for the style of numbered helmet and green frog cammies worn by Marines (as indicated by Marti in text). Note: I have sent relevant images to Ahmad. 4. Ahmad then brings group calmly through the canal toward Marines. Note: I'm going to tell him single file line is fine, unless you tell me they want it even slower, like one individual at a time. 5. Ahmad speaks codeword to Marines. Note: Codeword *not* yet known at this time. Awaiting further info on this. 6. Ahmad identifies for Marines all members of each group.*

Note: This could be challenging, as Ahmad will have just met the people in each group. And we expect 30+ people. Ahmad may be able to visually identify group members but may not be able to name all of them. An option may be for Ahmad to name all other group leaders, who in turn can then name members of their groups. Any clarification on what kind of identification of group members Ahmad will be expected to provide will be appreciated.

Our planned exfil time comes and goes. I'm trying to raise Marti, but he isn't answering my texts. When I call, his phone simply rings and rings. While we're trying to get in touch with him, Nick appears on a separate text exchange. I haven't heard from him since our unsuccessful attempt on the South Gate. He asks about a contact of his, Noorzai, who has a visa but no way to enter the airport. Noorzai is up at the North Gate. Any chance we could help him get inside HKIA? I explain that he's in luck. We have a group at the Abbey Gate, ready to go; that is, if Noorzai can get down there in time. Right as I'm passing along Ahmad's cell phone for Nick to give to Noorzai, Marti comes up on the group chat, responding to an hours-old message of mine in which I'd asked for an update on possible linkup times. He replies, *My guys are actively pulling groups still. I passed out for a bit. I'll know more once I'm back in the office.*

It's now coming up on four p.m., so getting late when Nick writes in the chat, *Noorzai spoke with Ahmad, planning to link up in 30 mins.*

Tell him to hurry, I reply. *Marines are getting ready for the pull.*

Ten minutes pass; then Marti comes back up in the chat. He requests another photograph of Ahmad. He asks us to be patient. He has several teams, all pulling people from the crowd. He apologizes and explains that he's waiting for a team to free up. Not long thereafter, Marti gets tired of waiting. He's going to go himself and writes, *On my way personally now.*

Ahmad posts an emoji of two hands praying.

Another couple of minutes pass. Then Marti writes, *Lead member make your way down into the canal to be recognized more easily.*

Ahmad: Ok. All should get into canal?

Marti: Carefully enter and be patient im on my way. My numbers on my helmet.

Ahmad: Ok.

Marti: 102.

(Again, Marti posts the photograph of his low-profile helmet with the numbers stenciled to a Velcro patch on its side.)

Another five minutes pass; then Ahmad writes, *In the canal sir.*

Then, on a separate chat, I check in with Nick on Noorzai's progress: *Exfil beginning now. Is he there?*

Nick: I think he's close, trying to get confirmation.

(Another five minutes pass.)

Nick: I can't raise him. Hoping that means he's near the gate so the jammers are doing it. Anything from Ahmad?

I tell Nick that he's in the canal awaiting the Marines. When I try to get in touch with Ahmad, to see if he's managed to link up with Noorzai, he isn't answering either. Then Nick gets a message from Noorzai, who writes, *The gate is very close. I saw Americans.* But that's it. Nothing else from Noorzai. Thirty minutes pass. It's nearly five p.m. Finally, I receive a text from Ahmad: *Hi.*

Are you in the airport? I ask.

Yes sir.

When I ask Ahmad about Noorzai, he writes, *He got there late. I was helping identify the 29 people while he might have called. I'm really sorry sir.*

Then Marti pops up on the chat: *I pulled all 29 personally.*

In that moment, it occurs to me that I never once mentioned to Marti that I'd served in the Marines. I feel grateful to him and proud of the Marines who are doing this work and tell him the same, listing the units I served with but also my class number at the Amphibious Reconnaissance School, which seems to be all he's interested in because he responds with his own class number: *ARS class March 07.*

To which I respond, *Loch Ness, baby. Proud to know you.*

Fuck that hill! he writes. *End of every fucking goddamn run! We hit it twice on some, fucking assholes!!*

Yep, I write. *Fuck that hill.*

Twenty minutes later, a suicide bomber detonates at the Abbey Gate. Thirteen Americans are killed, along with 150 Afghans. Marti survives, as do Ahmad and the others we've just pulled out. Noorzai also survives the blast. But he remains trapped on the wrong side of the gate.

ACT V

THE
FIFTH
ACT

May God reward the oppressed people of Afghanistan who fought the infidels and the oppressors for twenty years.

—TALIBAN SUPREME LEADER HAIBATULLAH AKHUNDZADA
DARUL ULOOM HAKIMAH MADRASSA, KANDAHAR
OCTOBER 31, 2021

SCENE I

An office, Camp Lejeune, North Carolina

<u>■■■■■■■■</u>

The day after the bomb goes off at Abbey Gate, a video begins circulating. It's of Marine Lieutenant Colonel Stuart Scheller. He sits at his desk wearing his camouflage utility uniform, the sleeves rolled tightly over his biceps. Scrawled on a dry-erase board behind him are notes from an earlier meeting, to include tactical symbols unintelligible to those who haven't served in or studied the military. Through a grimace, he says, "The baby boomers' turn is over. I demand accountability, at all levels. If we don't get it, I'm bringing it." His nearly five-minute post is forwarded to me by an old friend from the Marines, who is also a lieutenant colonel and who also remains on active duty. He writes, *If Stu has his job by the end of today, it'll be a miracle.*

In the video, Scheller calls out senior military leaders, including

Chairman of the Joint Chiefs of Staff General Mark Milley, Comman-
dant of the Marine Corps General David Berger, and Secretary of Defense Lloyd Austin. "People are upset because their senior leaders let
them down, and none of them are raising their hands and accepting
accountability or saying, 'We messed this up.'" But Scheller's remarks
go one step further than a simple demand for accountability. He goes
on to quote Thomas Jefferson, who said, "Every generation needs a
revolution."

When I finish watching the video, I'm not sure what to make of it.
My first instinct is to categorize it as a rant. If it wasn't clear already,
after the bombing at Abbey Gate it becomes evident that the Biden
administration has handled the evacuation of Afghanistan with an
exceptional degree of incompetence. Emotions are raw, so a rant—
even if inappropriate when delivered by an active-duty officer—seems
understandable. However, after more thought, I slowly realize that
what I've just watched is something else: an act of self-immolation.

My friend who sent me the video is proved right, and by the end of the day senior officers have swiftly relieved Scheller of his battalion command. The Marine Corps is very selective about which officers it grooms to become battalion commanders; the fact that Scheller held this posting means he was—before this incident—well regarded, a Marine with a future in the Corps. Furthermore, Scheller is seventeen years into a twenty-year career. At twenty years, he would have been eligible for retirement at half his base pay with other benefits, like health care for life. It takes him exactly four minutes and forty-five seconds to throw that all away. Scheller is a husband and a father. Why did he do this?

It's often been said that while America's military has spent the past twenty years at war, America itself has been at the mall. This has led to a massive civil-military divide. This botched withdrawal, in which active-duty as well as former members of the military are receiving hundreds of phone calls and texts daily from their Afghan allies and their families who are now left to fend for themselves against the Taliban, has only deepened this sense of alienation among so many who've served. This sense of alienation combined with an increased politicization of the US military is, for our democracy, a combustible mix.

In the eighteen months leading up to the Afghan withdrawal, we have witnessed a politicization of the US military with few precedents, with everything from General Mark Milley marching across Lafayette Park in his fatigues with President Trump, to the congressional testimony of senior officers—on subjects ranging from January 6 to right-wing extremism to critical race theory—becoming fodder for late-night cable news anchors who seek to position those in uniform on one side or the other of the Democratic-Republican divide. The US military is, historically and ostensibly, an apolitical organization, but this has never meant military members do not have political views. Of course they do. But the military stays out of politics because it practices a code of omertà. Scheller's video breaks that code.

The Marine Corps is a small community. Back when Scheller was a twentysomething lieutenant, he served in 1/8 a year after I did. My friend who sent me the video, the other lieutenant colonel I mentioned—he and I served in 1/8 together in Iraq. We also did our training together in Quantico, where we were in the same class as Lieutenant Colonel Richardella, who is the current commander of 1/8, and it's his Marines who are holding the line at HKIA when Scheller records his video. We all know one another. But fewer and fewer Americans know us.

The all-volunteer military has become isolated from broader American culture. The model of the citizen soldier that characterized the American military for generations has been replaced by a professional soldiering class, one that is increasingly closed off, insular, and subject to living in its own atomized reality—just like the rest of America does. This is dangerous.

The first presidential election I witnessed as a member of the military was George W. Bush versus Al Gore in 2000. I was in college, as a naval ROTC midshipman, and on Election Day I remember asking a Marine colonel who was a visiting fellow at my university whether he'd made it to the polls. In much the same way one might say, "I don't smoke" when offered a cigarette, he said, "Oh, I don't vote." His answer confused me at the time. He was a third-generation military officer, someone imbued with a strong sense of duty. He then explained that as a military officer he felt it was his obligation to remain apolitical. In his estimation, this included not casting a vote on who his commander in chief might be.

Although I don't agree that one's commitment to remaining apolitical while in uniform extends to not voting, I would over the years come across others who abstained from voting on similar grounds. That interaction served as an early lesson on the lengths some in the military would go to steer clear of politics. It also illustrated that those in uniform have, by definition, a different relationship to the president than civilians do. As that colonel saw it in 2000, he wouldn't be voting for his president but rather for his commander in chief, and he didn't feel it was appropriate to vote for anyone in his chain of command. As it turned out, the result of that election was contested. Gore challenged the result after Florida was called for Bush, and the dispute went all the way to the Supreme Court between the election and the inauguration, by which point Gore had conceded.

There are many ways to contest an election, some of which are far more reckless and unseemly than others, but our last two presidential elections certainly qualify. In 2016, Democrats contested Donald Trump's legitimacy based on claims of collusion between his campaign and Russia. In 2020, Republicans significantly escalated the level of contestation around the election with widespread claims of voter fraud, which ultimately erupted in rioting on January 6, 2021.

Today, dysfunction runs deep in American politics. While the images from January 6 remain indelible, the images of entire cities in red and blue states boarded up in the days before the 2020 presidential election should also concern us. If contested elections become the norm, then mass protests around elections become the norm, and if mass protests become the norm, then police and military responses to those protests will surely follow. This is a new normal we can ill afford. Little progress has been made to understand this cycle of contested elections we are trapped in, with the most recent attempt—the January 6 commission—receiving tepid support in Congress.

Destructive complexes are not new in American life. In his farewell address to the nation, President Dwight Eisenhower issued this warning: "In the councils of government, we must guard against the acquisition of unwarranted influence, whether sought or unsought, by the military-industrial complex. The potential for the disastrous rise of misplaced power exists and will persist."

Eisenhower, who in his military career had commanded Allied forces in Europe against the Nazis, delivered those remarks in January 1961, at the height of the Cold War, which had led to a drastic militarization of American society. In the more than sixty years since Eisenhower's address, the term "industrial complex" has been used to describe the self-justifying and self-perpetuating nature of various industries—medicine, entertainment, and education, to name a few. But it is the political incarnation that we are most dangerously mired in now. Just as the military-industrial complex threatened to undermine democracy in Eisenhower's time, the political-industrial complex threatens to undermine democracy in ours.

A 2020 analysis published in the *Harvard Business Review* by Katherine Gehl and Michael Porter describes this systemic threat succinctly: "Far from being 'broken,' our political system is doing precisely what it's designed to do. It wasn't built to deliver results in the public interest or to foster policy innovation, nor does it demand accountability for failure to do so. Instead, most of the rules that shape

day-to-day behavior and outcomes have been perversely optimized—
or even expressly created—by and for the benefit of the entrenched
duopoly at the center of our political system: the Democrats and the
Republicans (and the actors surrounding them), what collectively we
call the political-industrial complex."

This political-industrial complex includes not only legions of
campaign staffers, pollsters, consultants, and other party functionar-
ies, but also media (both traditional and nontraditional) that inspire
division because division keeps people engaged, keeps eyeballs on
screens, and so drives profit.

While average prime-time viewership across the top three cable
news channels had fallen by roughly a third from 2008 to 2014, the
advent of Donald Trump's candidacy and election caused viewership
to soar, with CNN clearing nearly $1 billion in profits in 2016. In the
lead-up to the 2020 presidential election, Fox News became the
highest-rated television channel during the prime-time hours of eight
to eleven p.m. This wasn't just on cable news. It became the highest-
rated channel in *all* of television.

The effects of this complex extend far outside politics. Today,
nearly every facet of life falls somewhere along the left-right political
spectrum. Every question we ask ourselves is shot through the lens of
politics. During the pandemic, for instance, I desperately wanted my
elementary school–aged children in the classroom, with their friends.
When speaking to other parents, did this fervent desire to see my children in the classroom, even as we grappled with the coronavirus,
make me a Trump supporter? A Republican?

I am also a veteran. When I tell my military buddies that prisoners
of war should never be slandered and that convicted war criminals

shouldn't be trotted out as national heroes, do they assume that I'm also a fan of the Green New Deal? A Democrat? The politicization of American life is swiftly becoming total, with virtually no opinion or thought existing outside the realm of partisan sorting.

In 1939, when America was emerging from the throes of the Great Depression, our military ranked nineteenth largest in the world, standing behind Portugal. The Second World War, and the Cold War that followed, epitomized what theorists call "total war," in which every facet of a society is mobilized. This was a departure from centuries past, when nations typically waged "limited war," relying on professional armies instead of the widespread enlistment of its citizenry and means of national production. One consequence of total war is that even nonmilitary parts of society become military targets: manufacturing, agriculture, energy, even civilian populations.

By the time Eisenhower delivered his address, total war had reached its zenith, as the development of civilization-ending nuclear weapons had made the human race's continued existence contingent on a precarious doctrine of "mutually assured destruction" between the United States and the Soviet Union.

One way to measure our current state of "total politics" is to look at the ballooning economics of presidential campaigns. In the 1980 presidential election, spending by Republicans and Democrats combined totaled $60 million ($190 million when adjusted for inflation). In 2020, filings show that the election cost $14.4 billion, which represents a seventy-five-times increase in spending.

While the military-industrial complex fed off the US-Soviet Cold War conflict, the political-industrial complex feeds off the left-right conflict. If the military-industrial complex led us into a paradigm of perpetual wars with little hope of victory and no end in sight (Korea, Vietnam, Iraq, Afghanistan), then the political-industrial complex has led us into a paradigm of perpetual campaigns in which our political class needs divisive issues to fight over more than it needs solutions to the issues themselves—crucial issues like gun control, immigration, and health care.

Our passions are being inflamed and manipulated for profit by a political-industrial complex that feeds off our basest fears of one another. Our experiment in democracy has worked when it appeals to the best in us, as opposed to the worst. Eisenhower recognized this, and it was that instinct he appealed to in each of us as he closed his farewell address: "Down the long lane of the history yet to be written America knows that this world of ours, ever growing smaller, must avoid becoming a community of dreadful fear and hate, and be, instead, a proud confederation of mutual trust and respect."

And if we do become a community of dreadful fear and hate?

In the Cold War, failure meant mutually assured destruction through nuclear war. It was an outcome that, fortunately, never arrived, though it's instructive that Eisenhower's farewell address came a little less than two years before the Cuban Missile Crisis, the closest humanity has ever come to nuclear annihilation. Today, we sit on a different sort of precipice. Are we entering an era where we hold elections in a nation so hopelessly divided that neither side is willing to accept defeat? In a democracy, that is the truest form of mutually assured destruction.

This takes us back to that colonel I knew in college and his conviction to stay out of politics. Increasingly, in military circles, this view has seemed to fall out of favor, particularly among retired officers. In 2016, for the first time in recent memory, we saw large speaking roles doled out to prominent retired military leaders at both parties' national conventions. This trend has accelerated in recent years, and in the 2020 elections we saw some retired flag officers (including the former heads of several high commands) writing and speaking out against Donald Trump in prominent media outlets, and others organizing against Joe Biden's agenda in groups like Flag Officers 4 America.

The US military is one of the most trusted institutions in our society, and so support from its leaders has become an increasingly valuable political commodity. If this trend of increased military politicization seeps into the active-duty ranks, it could lead to dangerous outcomes, particularly around elections, and specifically a presidential one.

Many commentators have already pointed out that it's likely that in 2024 (or even 2022) the losing party will cry foul, and it is also likely that their supporters will fill the streets, with law enforcement or even the military called in to manage those protests. It is not hard to imagine, then, with half the country claiming an elected leader is illegitimate, that certain military members who hold their own biases might begin to second-guess their orders. This might sound alarmist, but so long as political leaders continue to question the legitimacy of our president, some in our military might do the same.

Holding contested elections is like driving drunk. The drunk driver goes to the bar, has one too many, and often makes it home safely. They convince themselves in the morning that the night before wasn't that bad, that they can hold their liquor. Typically, a safe return will only reinforce the drunk driver's belief that they can get away with a little irresponsible behavior at the bar; that is, until they wrap their car around a telephone pole. So maybe we wrap our proverbial car around the telephone pole the first time or maybe it's the fifth time, but when bad behaviors become habits, the worst outcomes become inevitabilities.

Doubt around the legitimacy of elections is particularly dangerous when a republic has a large standing military, but also one that feels misunderstood or even betrayed by the society it serves, sentiments expressed by Scheller in his video. Does everyone feel like him? No, of course not. But after twenty years of war culminating in the botched evacuation of Kabul, I am hearing his sense of betrayal echoed by others.

So how we think about Scheller's video matters. It's important to understand that it was not so much a rant as an act of self-immolation. And acts of self-immolation, if not heeded, have historically preceded

cataclysmic breakdowns in society. Remember Mohamed Bouazizi, the Tunisian fruit vendor? Or Thích Quảng Đức, the Vietnamese monk? One inspired a rallying cry for the Arab Spring, and the other remains an iconic martyr of the Vietnam War. Read about them. You will notice that each burned for approximately four minutes and forty-five seconds.

SCENE II

The US Naval Academy

It's twenty years to the day since 9/11. As planned, Josh has flown up with his son, six-year-old Weston, and we're awake early getting ready to take our boys to the Navy versus Air Force football game. Josh arrived the night before, from Wilmington—not far from Camp Lejeune—where he settled after medically retiring from the Marine Corps. Had it not been for his leg wound, I always imagined that Josh would've stuck around the Corps and tended to the organization; he would've made a fine general. Instead, he's made himself into a successful businessman. He once joked with me that he'd done every quintessential thing a person could do as an American: he'd gone to war; he'd started a family; he'd built and taken a business public. He laughed telling me this, but also admitted that he wasn't certain what came next.

The night he arrived, after we'd put the boys to bed, he and I had stayed up late, talking over drinks about this very same subject. Specifically, we were discussing Afghanistan's future, but that conversation had a subtext; it was entwined with what would come next for each of us now that our war was at last over. This summer, about a week before Kabul fell, Josh had sent me a video. It was of a battalion of Afghan commandos as they prepared for one of their final offensives, a desperate helicopter assault into Lashkar Gah, the then-besieged capital of Helmand Province. The video was shot in dark, midnight tonalities. The heavily armed commandos marched in formation out to the helicopters that awaited them on the tarmac. In Dari they shouted, "God is great!" followed by "Long live Afghanistan!" It had been years since Josh had been in Afghanistan, but he confessed that seeing that video made him long to return. He felt like he should've been loading onto those helicopters. Watching that video had made me want to return too. Or, put another way, it had reminded me that no matter how far my life progressed beyond the war—in family, in work, in friendship—the war always had its hold over me, calling me back. Josh was, as we sat at my dinner table, giving me a bit of shit for the video I'd sent to him in response, which was a favorite scene from *The Princess Bride*. It's from the end of the movie, after the Spanish swordsman Inigo Montoya has killed the six-fingered man and avenged his father's death. He turns to his good friend Westley, the stable boy turned pirate, and says wistfully, "You know, it's very strange. I have been in the revenge business so long, now that it's over I don't know what to do with the rest of my life." To which Westley replies, "Have you ever considered piracy? You'd make a wonderful Dread Pirate Roberts." Josh was class of 2001 out of the Naval Academy. He was in the revenge business for a long time.

After the bombing at Abbey Gate, our ability to get Afghans into the airport came to a standstill; however, the number of Afghans trying to leave only seemed to increase. As it became obvious that the window for departures had narrowed to a sliver, those Afghans who'd thought to bide their time until conditions at the airport improved now seemed willing to take risks they wouldn't have considered a week before. Josh was curious how the final few days of the evacuation had gone from my perspective. Most of my efforts, I explained, now centered on helping a family Admiral Mullen was trying to get out. They were nine in total, to include four small children. The patriarch of the family, who I'll call Aziz, had worked at the US embassy. His brother, who'd worked as a driver for a senior government minister, had already been assassinated by the Taliban, while the minister himself had slunk away, boarding a plane out of HKIA in the early days of the evacuation.

Aziz primarily sends me voice notes. I play a few of them for Josh, beginning with one that Aziz recorded on the night of Abbey Gate. He had been nearby, like so many others trying to get into the airport, when the bomb went off. "Hello, sir, I hope you're doing good," Aziz begins, with a tremor in his voice. "We just moved back and are trying to go somewhere else. We don't want to get caught by Taliban, because they are looking everywhere, place by place, home by home, street by street, looking for us. We don't want to be recognized by them. I was so close to that explosion and the mark of blood is all over on my clothes. All the family is so scared. Sir, I am waiting for your next call. If it's possible, sir, it would be so good to, um, uh . . ." Aziz stumbles over his words for a moment before regaining enough composure to say, "I'm not in a condition to talk clearly. I can get close or near to the airport. If it's possible to pick us up, it would be good. For now, all the family is in very bad condition. They're so scared. Kids are so scared. Everyone is in bad condition."

I play Josh another message from Aziz, this one from only a couple of days ago. After the final flight of Americans left the airport in Kabul, Aziz traveled north, with all nine of his family members crammed into a taxi, to Mazar-i-Sharif, where his family and others are hiding in a safe house, awaiting a flight that may or may not come. The safe house isn't really a house but a wedding hall rented out at an exorbitant rate by private donors who are footing the bill for this evacuation. He's been there about a week. There's about a week's worth of funding left to pay for the safe house. The Taliban have been to his home in Kabul. Once that funding runs out, if he hasn't gotten out on a flight, he'll have nowhere to go. Aziz's message comes with a video as he films the squalor of the wedding hall, the children wandering around aimlessly, the families sleeping beneath the stairways and others sleeping in the open hall itself, on filthy carpets, with empty bottles of water and other bits of trash strewn about. "Please, sir, please," he says, "I want you to help me, my family, my kids. This is not a safe place. I'm going to shut down my cell phone and put it somewhere. I'm just completely lost. I don't know what to do."

Josh asks whether I think Aziz will get out. I describe some recent complications. Kam Air, the largest Afghan-based private airline, is the only one the Taliban will allow to fly. A few nights before, Aziz's flight had been cleared. But in a corrupt scheme, the Kam Air pilots had offered their seats to the highest bidder, in effect double-selling the flight for millions in profit. This caused a delay. Then, once that problem was resolved, the flight was again cleared, but at the last moment a local Taliban commander blocked its departure because he had not received a payout. The day after that, it was an issue with Qatari landing clearances in Doha. Currently, the US State Department was holding up the flight with a demand that every Afghan on board have a passport, to include children older than age one. Aziz's children don't have passports. After enumerating these difficulties, Josh asks how often I'm receiving messages like this from Aziz.

I tell him about every day.

Then he asks, "Are you doing all right?"

The next morning, we're in the car with the boys, and we're not talking about Afghanistan anymore. We're talking about the football game, and the boys are excited. Neither have ever been to a game, and neither have been to Annapolis before. We arrive on campus early, so the boys can walk around. We stroll past the faculty housing, old Victorian bungalows with rocking chairs on wraparound porches and shaded verandas and freshly manicured lawns. Heads turn as tight formations of midshipmen march past. The boys want to look at every cannon, every gun, and every statue. Then we arrive at the statue of Tecumseh. A placard nearby reads, "The original wooden image was sent to the Naval Academy in 1866 after being salvaged from the wreck of the old ship of the line 'Delaware,' which had been sunk at Norfolk during the Civil War to prevent her from falling into Confederate hands. The builders of the 'Delaware' intended the figurehead to portray Tamanend, the great chief of the Delawares, a lover of peace and friend of William Penn. But to the midshipmen of the period, there was nothing in the name of Tamanend to strike the imagination. The effigy was also known by various other names—Powhatan, King Philip, and finally Tecumseh—a great warrior and thus heroic and appropriate to the midshipmen."

Josh explains to the boys (and to me) that the original figurehead was made of wood. This bronze Tecumseh came later, a replica erected in the 1930s. The boys seem disappointed by this, but Josh explains that when the class of 1891 raised the money to build a permanent, bronze effigy of Tecumseh, they made sure a portion of the original would remain. They ripped out the wooden heart and the wooden brain of the original Tecumseh and placed those in the bronze replica. Like Frankenstein, say the boys. Yes, like Frankenstein.

Tecumseh Monument, U. S. Naval Academy, Annapolis, Md.

Pennies litter the base of Tecumseh's granite pedestal. Josh explains that Tecumseh is also known as the "God of 2.0," the passing grade point average at the academy. Legend has it that if you say a prayer to Tecumseh and give an offering of a penny—by flicking it up into the quiver of arrows Tecumseh wears on his back—he will grant you good luck in your exams. But Tecumseh's quiver is quite high. The boys climb onto our shoulders. They have gathered a few pennies each, which they toss into the sky.

We cross the brick courtyard that divides Tecumseh's statue from Bancroft Hall. Built in a beaux arts style with a sloping copper mansard roof and tidy dormer windows, this is the vast continuous dormitory that houses the midshipmen. Contained within Bancroft Hall is Memorial Hall, which is built atop a marble staircase that ascends from the central Rotunda. Weston runs ahead of us as we climb the stairs toward Memorial Hall. He then stops in his tracks near the top. Crudely stitched on a large blue flag are the words *Don't Give Up the Ship*, which Weston is reading as his father takes him by the hand and leads him inside.

Beneath that flag, located in the center of Memorial Hall, is a list of names inside a glass case: the Naval Academy graduates killed in America's wars. Josh and I have several shared friends listed among them, to include J. P. Blecksmith, who was in the same class in Quantico as Chris Richardella and me. He was killed on a rooftop in Fallujah, in 2004. Also on this list is Megan McClung, the first female academy graduate killed in combat. She was engaged to a friend of mine when she died, in 2006. Among these names, the one that figures most prominently to us is Doug Zembiec. Doug is the reason we're friends.

I met Doug in 2002. He was second-in-command of the Amphibious Reconnaissance School when I was a student there. Two weeks after starting the grueling course, my classmates and I were given a night off. We went to a restaurant nearby, in Virginia Beach, where we spotted Captain Zembiec and his then-girlfriend, later wife, Pam, having dinner. We ordered them each a drink, on us. A few minutes later, as they were leaving the restaurant, Doug came to our table with a waiter in tow. A half dozen of us sat at the table and the waiter carried the same number of Jäger shots on a tray, plus one extra. Doug snatched the extra shot, held it aloft, and said some things about us training to be among the fiercest warriors in the world, about us slaying America's enemies, and that the luckiest and most honorable of us would all meet in Valhalla one day. (I would come to learn this was typical Doug-speak.) And then, in a way that would be utterly obnoxious if it wasn't coming from him, he raised the glass just a little higher and said, "Marine Reconnaissance, men want to be us and women want to be with us!" and we all drank. Love him or hate him, that was Doug. (I loved him.)

Josh's story of how he met Doug was, actually, more colorful, and even more quintessentially Doug. It was two years later, in Fallujah, and Josh was a young lieutenant leading a heavy machine-gun platoon mounted in Humvees. His platoon of about forty Marines was assigned to help Doug's dismounted company of more than one hundred enter a heavily contested neighborhood. It was the middle of the night when the two linked up on the side of the road. Josh was sitting in the front passenger seat of his Humvee when Doug approached with a map and flashlight. Doug explained how he wanted Josh to take point for his company as they advanced. After Doug laid out his plan, Josh said, "No problem, sir. If you want to hang in the back, I'm happy to lead your company for you."

Doug, who'd been an All-American wrestler at Navy, didn't appreciate Josh's insubordinate remark. He made a quick and casual threat of physical violence, along the lines of dragging Josh out of his

Humvee and pounding some sense into him. The young lance corporal driving Josh's truck promptly confronted Doug. "Sir," he said,
leaning over his steering wheel, "if you want to fight our lieutenant,
you're going to have to fight all of us."

This stopped Doug in his tracks. "What's that?"

The lance corporal repeated the platoon's position.

"Are you saying if I lay a hand on your lieutenant, you're going to
fight me, a captain of Marines?"

"Yes, sir," said Josh's driver. "You touch him, you fight all of us."

Doug considered Josh for another moment, as if looking at him
for the first time. He was impressed. "What'd you say your name was
again, lieutenant?"

Josh repeated his name.

"Okay," said Doug. "I'm going to remember that. And I'm Zembiec, like *beck*, not Zem-*biack*. If you're alive after this, I'm going to
find you. We're going to be friends." Josh then took point for Doug's
company, leading them into Fallujah. And Doug kept his word, finding Josh after the battle. From then on, he took a special interest in
Josh, in much the same way he took a special interest in me, which
Josh and I both knew because Doug later made a point of introduc-
ing us.

Like I said, he's the reason we're friends.

I met Doug in 2002.

Josh met him in 2004.

Doug was killed in Baghdad, shot in the face on a raid with a
group of CIA-sponsored Iraqi commandos, in 2007. This wasn't a lot
of time. Today, he's buried in Arlington, just a few plots away from
Tubes.

As we're standing by the list that contains Doug's name, a man, perhaps a little younger than us, with what appears to be his young wife, or his girlfriend, begins to read from the list. It doesn't take long before he comes to Doug. "This guy, Zem-*biack*, now he was a legend. I've heard about him. He was a wrestler here, an All-American. The 'Lion of Fallujah,' that's what the Marines called him."

Each year, the Corps gives a leadership trophy named in Doug's honor.

Josh and I step away, until we're out of earshot. "That's pretty funny," he says. "You know Doug's up in Valhalla, laughing his ass off that we're down here having to overhear people talk about what a legend he was."

Josh is right. The Doug who brought us shots of Jäger in Virginia Beach, who threatened to fight Josh in Fallujah, who was messy and obnoxious and a true believer and a true friend, would have found it fitting that we lived and he died in battle and that the world is still telling stories about him as we simply get older. In the days after Doug was killed, when the pain around the loss was acute, many of us who'd been his friends found some solace in believing that Doug likely would've been okay with dying the way that he did, on a raid, in a desperate exchange of gunfire, leading a group of commandos. The more time that's passed, the more I've wondered if this was actually true. Would he have been okay knowing that he'd never get to see his daughter grow up? Or that he had to leave behind his wife? Or that his parents would outlive him? I want to believe what Josh says, that Doug is looking down at us from Valhalla (or wherever he is) and laughing. I want to believe that, in the end, the time you have means less than what you do with it or how you're remembered; it's pretty to think so.

Soon it's lunchtime and the boys are hungry. We walk them off the academy grounds, to a burger place on the Annapolis waterfront. The game starts in a couple of hours. Alumni and boosters tether their boats to the marina. Their turned-up stereos only add to the celebratory air. Not long after we settle at our table and order our meal, my phone rings. It's Admiral Mullen, so I take it. Given the music blaring in the background, he asks where I am. I explain that I'm at his alma mater to watch Navy beat Air Force. He's at home, in Pennsylvania, and adds that from what he's heard about the season so far, it's likely going to be the other way around. He's checking in to see whether there's been any progress on Aziz's flight. When we last spoke, the State Department's new requirement on passports was preventing Aziz's departure. A contact of mine—a former special forces soldier turned McKinsey consultant—is hopeful that he can get the State Department to waive this requirement for Aziz's family, but we're still awaiting confirmation. This is what I pass along to the admiral. He asks me to keep him posted and we hang up.

"It's pretty fucked up that not even Mullen can get people out," says Josh.

To which I agree.

"Do you think you're going to get this guy out?"

"I don't know."

"I hope that you do."

I tell Josh that the prospect of having to leave people like Aziz behind has dredged up a lot of old memories, specifically about Tubes. And about Momez. Josh understands. He has a story of his own, one that in certain ways parallels my story in Shewan. A year after Tubes was killed, Josh's team of Marines was advising the same battalion of Afghan commandos that I'd advised, performing this mission alongside the very same team of special forces soldiers that I'd worked with. Toward the end of his deployment—on the mission before he was wounded in the leg—he'd planned a helicopter raid into a remote part of northwestern Afghanistan known for the type of poppy cultivation that was funding the Taliban insurgency. This mission, which was co-sponsored by the Drug Enforcement Agency, and which even had a former Marine turned DEA agent participating, had flown in three helicopters to a village deep inside Taliban-held territory.

After landing, the raid force had met sporadic resistance but was able to destroy a vast quantity of opium and seize key figures in both the insurgency and the drug trade. With their objectives met, Josh had called in the helicopters to exfiltrate them. The village was in a canyon, built against a sheer cliff face. The landing zone was tight, requiring the helicopters to touch down facing the cliff face. As the helicopters landed, their rotors would kick up blinding swirls of dust. So the pilots knew that they would have to make a blind, ninety-degree turn on takeoff before ascending above the dust cloud and out of the canyon. They successfully performed the maneuver when they inserted the raid force. Then, on exfiltration, one of the pilots had landed slightly askew. When he took off with his portion of the raid force and turned ninety degrees, he was still partially facing the cliff. His helicopter crashed. Josh had been in a different helicopter and ordered the raid force to turn around. They landed on the valley floor.

They had a number of wounded, a number of dead, and the remaining Taliban were consolidating to launch a counterattack. For hours, they fought at the crash site. Eventually, Josh was able to get his wounded evacuated. But they couldn't get out the dead, which totaled ten, including the pilots, one of the special forces soldiers who was a mutual friend of ours, and the lead DEA agent. They were low on water, low on food, and low on ammunition. Then, after the better part of a day, a contingent of US Air Force pararescue men finally arrived; pararescue men, with their specialized training and equipment, are world-renowned experts in personnel recovery. After a quick survey of the scene, the pararescue men determined that, given the violence of the crash as well as the continued threat posed by the Taliban, a recovery of the bodies wasn't viable. They advised that Josh and the remainder of his force should leave. The pararescue men made some comments about calling in an air strike to incinerate the wreckage, and that this was the best outcome they could hope for. Josh refused. The pararescue men then flew out on the helicopters they came in on. A few hours later, and still without a plan, Josh heard that a contingent of US Army Rangers in the area had volunteered to help. They flew in on helicopters of their own, and despite having no formal training in personnel recovery, the Rangers (many of them not much older than twenty) got to work. Several hours later, they'd managed to extract the remaining bodies from the wreckage.

Josh could've left, but he didn't; I know this about him.

And so I also know that he hasn't had to live with the questions I've asked after leaving someone behind, in the way we'd left Momez behind in Shewan. Which leads me to wonder whether he understands a certain fear I've been holding on to, how I'm afraid that this botched withdrawal from Afghanistan is only going to leave me, and others like me, saddled with another set of regrets. Or questions. Of what *should've* or *could've* happened.

We've eaten our lunch. The boys are getting restless. Weston tugs at Josh and asks how much longer until the football game. Josh checks his watch; it's time. We pay the check and head toward the stadium. When we arrive outside, the parking lot is filled with tailgaters, filled with class reunions, and filled with midshipmen enjoying a precious day off. Like me, Josh doesn't come from a military family. He's a native of Dallas and has told me how isolated he felt at Annapolis, particularly during his early years, when he feared he might have made a mistake. I asked him once why he came to the academy and joined the Marine Corps. His answer was simple: "I read a book." That book, James Webb's *Fields of Fire*, is about a Marine rifle platoon in Vietnam. It's led by Second Lieutenant Robert E. Lee Hodges, who in many ways is a stand-in for Webb, an academy graduate himself who fought in Vietnam, was decorated, and went on to serve as secretary of the navy and a senator from Virginia. Josh added, "At eighteen, I wanted to *be* Hodges."

Standing outside the stadium, crammed shoulder to shoulder with today's midshipmen, I wonder if any of them want to be us, or at least the younger versions of us. When Josh offered to get these tickets, the Afghan withdrawal hadn't yet occurred. I doubt we would've come had we known that we wouldn't be marking the twenty-year anniversary of 9/11 so much as acknowledging our recent, unconditional defeat at the hands of the Taliban.

We find our seats.

A display of fighter jets flies low overhead.

Navy SEALs parachute from the sky, landing on the fifty-yard line.

The Brigade of Midshipmen marches through the stadium tunnel, clad in white, nearly four thousand strong, with the fluted guidons of their respective companies—A, B, C, D, and so forth—fluttering at the front right of each column. An announcer gives the names and hometowns of the brigade leadership as they take the field. Applause echoes through the stadium. A brass band plays the national anthem. Our boys are wide-eyed, standing on their seats, hands over their hearts.

I find myself again thinking about Hodges. About Josh. About the midshipmen. Our boys might want to be like the midshipmen, but I doubt the midshipmen want to be like us, particularly on this day. I can't blame them. Who wants to be at the end of a thing—particularly something that's gone as poorly as a lost war? No, we prefer beginnings.

Kickoff, and the game begins.

Yards are gained. Yards are lost. In no time at all, the admiral is proven correct, and the midshipmen fall several touchdowns behind the Air Force cadets. The boys are disappointed. Their wondrous, wide-eyed stares have narrowed to slits. Aren't the midshipmen always supposed to win? Isn't Navy the best? Doesn't it beat Air Force and Army? Doesn't it beat everyone?

We explain. Some years are better than others.

Not long after the half, we decide to beat traffic and leave early. Exhausted from the big day they've had, the two little boys stagger across the parking lot toward the car like a couple of drunken sailors. They're already falling asleep as we seat-belt them into the back. I see that I have a few missed text messages. My contact who is working Aziz's case, the special forces soldier turned McKinsey consultant, writes, *We really need help pushing the State Department to engage with us. They aren't answering phones or emails. It's absurd. We can't sustain ground operations that much longer.*

Then, on a separate thread, I have a message from Aziz, who writes, *When I'm receiving message from you it gives me hope to live, sir. I hear about the Qatar plane in Mazar.*

I show both messages to Josh. He asks, "What's the Qatar plane in Mazar?"

I explain that it's a privately funded flight slated to land in Qatar, but that the State Department won't clear the manifest. Only days ago, US Central Command was clearing the manifests, but now that the war has ended—or at least entered another act—the State Department has taken over this responsibility, and any manifest that Central Command had authorized before now has to be re-cleared by State, and State is using a different set of criteria than the US military.

We're driving back toward Washington as I continue to recount to Josh the ins and outs of this bureaucratic web that has ensnared Aziz and his family. I don't know Aziz. I've never met him. He's just a guy who leaves me voice notes asking for help that I'm unable to give. A certain degree of emotion must be coming through my voice because Josh interjects, saying, "I get it. It's frustrating. But you're doing all you can." I glance over at him in the passenger seat.

Yes, I want to help Aziz. But I also want to protect myself. I don't want to have the conversation in which we tell Aziz that we have to give up, that the money's run out, that he and his family are on their own. I don't want to have to live with that. And Josh doesn't know what it's like to live with those types of regrets. When he was confronted with leaving someone behind, he'd refused. Despite the wounds he lives with, he hasn't had to live with that type of second-guessing.

I tell him this.

He listens patiently, allowing me to finish. Then he says, "There were originally supposed to be four helicopters on that mission. Did you know that?"

I shake my head; no, I didn't know that.

"One of the four had a mechanical issue right before we left. We had to enact our bump plan, going from four helicopters to three.

We'd been planning this raid for weeks. The guys who got left back at base were pretty upset at the time. Some of them were upset with me because they felt I should have bumped the DEA agents off the mission. They didn't have the same tactical experience as us. But the lead agent, Mike, he'd served in the Marines. He and his guys had worked hard on developing this mission, and I felt they'd earned the right to come."

But Josh wasn't responsible for the helicopter crash. It wasn't a decision he'd made that caused that tragedy. He hears me out but disagrees.

"When I chose to keep Mike on the mission," he says, "and when we went from four helicopters down to three, it meant I placed Mike in what had been my seat. I was supposed to have been on that helicopter that crashed."

I apologize to Josh.

Specifically, I apologize for not understanding that he was experiencing America's end in Afghanistan in much the same way that I was, that each of us carries the weight of certain regrets, that we hide these old wounds. Until we can't. He neither accepts nor refuses my apology.

It sits between us in the car for a moment. Then he says, "Do you know what Mike's full name was?"

I don't.

"Special Agent Michael Weston." He turns toward the back seat, where his son, Weston, lies sleeping next to mine. "Someday," Josh says, "he'll understand what his name means."

EPILOGUE

A refugee camp, Doha, Qatar

A video arrives sometime in the night. It is from Aziz. I'd known the day before that he and his family had been manifested on a flight. But they had been manifested on many flights. And I'd often stayed up late, only to be disappointed when they didn't take off. I had quit staying up late, and so am asleep when this video arrives.

The room is small, with beds pushed into every corner. His daughter, not much younger than my own, plays with a paddleball on the bed. She is surrounded by other toys. I don't see Aziz, as he's holding the camera. There is only his voice. "Hello, sir. How are you?" he begins. "I hope you are doing good. We are in Qatar camp, so . . ." His son toddles into the frame; reaching into a pot, he pulls out a fist of blue Play-Doh that he holds up to the camera. Aziz laughs, and I realize that I've never heard Aziz laugh before. He continues, "So we got all this stuff for our kids, lots of playing stuff. Also everything, sir, everything. I have no idea how to thank . . ." And his voice breaks and trails off again.

He turns the camera and I can see his wife. She wears a long gray dress down to her ankles. Her face and patient smile are framed by a tightly worn hijab. Methodically, she unpacks their family into the cramped but clean confines of the room, which is like a hospital room in its sterility and efficient use of space. Emptied care packages of toiletries and towels, bottled water and packaged food like Cheez-Its and granola bars—it is all littered across the beds. Aziz takes his camera to show me this heaping pile of stuff.

Joy inflects his voice.

"For such a help, for such a mercy, for such a service, I have no idea how to thank. But I'm thankful of everyone, of every single person of US America, because we never dreamed such a thing. Their love. Their mercy. Thank you. Thank you for everything."

Not Helen's face, nor Paris was in
fault;
But by the gods was this destruction
brought.

—VIRGIL, *THE AENEID*

ACKNOWLEDGMENTS

My gratitude to PJ Mark, who first suggested this book; to Scott Moyers, whose unflagging support allowed its scope to change; and to Mia Council, who skillfully shepherded it through production. I'd also like to thank my children, for always understanding. And Lea Carpenter, for all she helps me understand.

LIST OF ILLUSTRATIONS